THE QUEEN BEE

Embody Your Truth & Live Fully Expressed

DONNA BOND STACIE COOPER DANIELLE DAWSON
DR. MARION GIBBON ANNA KOSKINARIS
JUDY MCNUTT NATALIE MURRAY MICOLE NOBLE
KAYLEIGH O'KEEFE JOY PADDISON ROBIN TOFT
PAMELA VATRANO KIRASTOULIS MEREDITH WILKIE
SONJA WÜTHRICH

THE QUEEN BEE © 2023 Soul Excellence Publishing

All Rights Reserved. Apart from any fair dealing for the purposes of research or private study, or criticism or review, as permitted under the Copyright, Designs and Patents Act 1988, this publication may only be reproduced, stored or transmitted, in any form or by any means, with the prior permission in writing of the copyright owner, or in the case of the reprographic reproduction in accordance with the terms of licenses issued by the Copyright Licensing Agency. Enquiries concerning reproduction outside those terms should be sent to the publisher.

Print ISBN: 979-8-9873454-8-1

Ebook ISBN: 979-8-9873454-9-8

Contents

Introduction Kayleigh O'Keefe	vii
1. Donna Bond *Spiritual Ambition: Activating the Soul's Code Toward Entelechy*	1
About the Author	11
2. Stacie Cooper *Rebirth into Motherhood*	13
About the Author	27
3. Danielle Dawson *Finding the Missingness: Shame as a Gateway to Deep Love and Connection*	29
About the Author	37
4. Carol DeFrancisco *Finding Your Beauty*	39
About the Author	51
5. Dr. Marion Gibbon *As in Nature, the End Makes Way for a New Beginning*	53
About the Author	63
6. Anna Koskinaris *Be True to Yourself, Live in Authenticity, and Become Your Own Heroine*	65
About the Author	77
7. Judy McNutt *Embody Your Intuition, Change Your Life*	79
About the Author	91
8. Natalie Murray *Dare to Become a 'Fully Evolved' Woman*	93
About the Author	105
9. Micole Noble *Being a Force for Enlightenment and Creation: My Journey from Dragonfly to Honeybee*	107
About the Author	117
10. Kayleigh O'Keefe *The Quest for Intimacy: From Worker Bee to Queen Bee*	119
About the Author	127
11. Joy Paddison *Finding Joy*	129
About the Author	141

12. Robin Toft — 143
    Becoming Love in Action
    About the Author — 153
13. Pamela Vatrano Kirastoulis — 155
    Tapping Into Your Divine Feminine Beauty
    About the Author — 163
14. Meredith Wilkie — 165
    Life on the Edge of Death
    About the Author — 175
15. Sonja Wüthrich — 177
    Soul Communication Excellence: The Treasure of Our Soul

About the Author — 191
Acknowledgments — 193
About Soul Excellence Publishing — 195
About Feminine Mastery — 197

In loving memory of **Cyndie Loven Fullenkamp**

1964-2022

Creator of Feminine Mastery

A Queen Bee and Guide For Each of Us Walking the Path of the Divine Feminine

May this book honor her legacy and inspire more women around the globe to awaken to their true calling

Introduction

Kayleigh O'Keefe

Cyndie Loven Fullenkamp (1964–2022), the creator of Feminine Mastery, came into my life through a Google search. The specific phrase I entered that fateful Friday night from my downtown San Francisco apartment was "women's retreat Hawaii." Just two weeks later, I found myself on the lush island of Maui, a spiritual vortex and the place where Cyndie had received the wisdom of the divine feminine archetypes, which she brings forth in her book *True Calling: Awaken the Power of Your True Self*. Now, I always heed the inner whisper telling me to search for something seemingly random on the internet!

My experience on the island would spark an inner awakening that had been long brewing beneath the surface, ever since my youth where I cherished my faith, loved writing page after page in my notebook, and intuitively picked up on the subtitles ever present in the world around me. My innate curiosity for our inner lives and God eventually took a backseat to the more pressing matters of the world that seemed to value prestige and elitism. Yet, while I played the game of life well, as I saw it at the time, by graduating from a top school, securing a job in management consulting, and making it my mission to be promoted the fastest, I knew deep within that my *true calling* was well beyond my present reality.

I met Cyndie at a time when my life looked, from the outside, the best it had ever been. I had received the largest commission check of my life, was responsible for building a commercial team, loved my downtown apartment and specifically its built-in bookshelves and stained glass windows mixed with its modern conveniences, and was being groomed to be a future female tech COO or CEO. Within, though, my light had dimmed and I felt myself in a state of mimic, copying the goals, means, and ways of the world around me.

The retreat softened my heart and gave me a new vocabulary from which to understand the various parts of myself. I began to observe how I could play with the divine feminine archetypes and call on them in certain situations to awaken my brightest, truest self. I continued on with Cyndie, working with her one-on-one to use the divine feminine archetypes to support my new role at the tech company I was working for at the time. A year later, I would return to Maui for the next retreat, this time with my girlfriend. After that Cyndie and I would work one-on-one to help me to bring forth Soul Excellence, my vision—and now premier publishing company—designed to help people express their inner transformations and evolutions through life. "Let's uncork Kayleigh!" she would often say to me as she guided me through my own journey of self-expression. I am forever grateful for how she saw me and what she sparked within me.

One year ago I received a call out of the blue from Cyndie's husband, Jon. "Cyndie has cancer and has just a few months to live." I was shocked. I knew she had been unwell, but clearly, I had been in the dark about the extent of what was really happening.

A few weeks later, I made the trip out to Del Mar and met with Cyndie in person. I walked through the door of the hillside home she was spending her final days in and was drawn once more to her crystalline blue eyes, which had not lost their sparkle even as the rest of her body showed signs of the toll the disease was taking on her. I gently embraced her tiny frame, and we took up residence for the afternoon on the couch, sharing stories from the past and planning for the future of Feminine Mastery. Cyndie had asked me to carry on Feminine Mastery, and I was there to have her talk me through her vision. I opened up my laptop and we ran through a task list, mostly of sharing website passwords and canceling software subscriptions. Anytime I broached the subject of a future vision—how would you like to see Feminine Mastery carried on?—Cyndie went quiet. Whether she kept on living on this planet or not, she told me, her heart had moved on to other creative endeavors, including the writing of a fiction novel and the building of her dream beach home. It was time for Feminine Mastery, a community of over thirty thousand women worldwide, to evolve.

As I reflected on how best to carry on the legacy of Feminine Mastery, it seemed obvious that the best way for me to do that was to bring together women who have been touched by Cyndie's work (whether through knowing her personally, reading her book, taking her quiz, or taking an online course) and invite them to share their own experience of awakening to the power of their true selves.

Over the past few years, I have birthed a community-based publishing company, Soul Excellence Publishing, designed to help individuals share their stories of personal growth and transformation in bestselling books. It made perfect sense that I would bring together women from around the globe to write a book together. The title instantly appeared in my mind: *The Queen Bee: Embody Your Truth and Live Fully Expressed.*

One of the five Divine Feminine Archetypes, the Honeybee, is "your creative power center allowing you to manifest your desire and bring any idea to fruition. She fosters loyalty and your commitment to serving your family, community, and higher source….On a quest to create greater prosperity for all, the Honeybee faithfully honors the inherent gifts offered by each person." I knew that we needed to come together, use our creative gifts, share our stories, and send the ripple effect out around the globe.

And so, the book you hold in your hands was born.

The last three years have been a portal for massive awakenings around the globe. For many of us, the illusion of "the outer way" has lifted and the truth of "the inner way" has permeated our being. The women in this book have courageously, faithfully followed the inner whispers of their hearts to reclaim their sovereignty and take their rightful seat as the queen of their kingdom. And collectively, we are creating kingdoms of beauty, truth, love, and a deep respect for our shared humanity.

I invite you to enjoy this book as a meditation, as a portal of possibilities. I invite you to connect with the women who have heeded the call to bear witness to the awakening that is rippling around the planet.

You are invited to join us on Facebook in the Feminine Mastery Inner Circle (whenever you are reading this book) to hear from the authors who will be sharing their stories and reflections on video as well.

https://www.facebook.com/groups/femininemasteryinnercircle

Are you ready to embody your truth and live fully expressed?

With love,

Kayleigh O'Keefe

Founder, Soul Excellence Publishing

ONE

Donna Bond

SPIRITUAL AMBITION: ACTIVATING THE SOUL'S CODE TOWARD ENTELECHY

> "If you're in the mess, you're on the path."
>
> —Kelly Notaras

I am still not sure what I'm doing here. Here in Central America in the rainforest of Costa Rica. In a home we built on land that was gifted to us. I am surrounded by my many beautiful belongings. My beloved books, statues of deities, and colorful boxes of oracle cards. *Archetypes* from Caroline Myss, *Keepers of the Light* by Kyle Gray, and *The Enchanted Map* by Colette Baron Reid, to name a few. All displayed on offer, dotted with crystals shining their magic. Rose quartz, labradorite, fluorite, amethyst, aquamarine, and white quartz.

The house plants and orchids stand holding a vibrant vibration of life-boasting color and strength emitting their aliveness into the room. From my desk, I'm gazing out the huge slider onto the jungle, the expansive ocean view, and the hazy white horizon. Today it's harder to make out the Osa Peninsula, the mist hanging like a veil keeping me separate from the invisible worlds. Regardless, it's all beautiful and luscious, alive and still, quiet and deafening, peaceful yet active. It's divinely organized chaos. It's perfectly orchestrated disorder. I don't know what I'm doing here.

And, I am getting more comfortable with that.

It's not my imagination that the universe wants me here. God wants me here. All the barriers and obstacles swept away literally as if the Red Sea was being parted. My only role to play was Trust. A giant act of surrender.

I didn't want the land. It was a sell job to convince me. The humidity of the tropics. Bugs as big as me. Buckets of endless rain. Rivers. Crocodiles. Snakes. Jungle. Two and a half acres of land. She gifted it to us. Honestly, I felt a little pissed. This is not my dream. This is not my plan. This is not my bag, baby. I'm much better suited in a pair of high heels and a Louis Vuitton.

"Let's build a house, let's build a house, let's build a house," sang my life-long surfer husband. he dreamed of waking, looking out the window to check the surf, and heading down to his own private beach, Playa Tortuga, where there is zero competition for waves.

"We don't have any money to build a house, my love. *When the money falls out of the sky, then we'll build a house.*" From my lips to God's ears—his dad died. We got an inheritance. We built the house. My very frugal husband, who is pretty tight with the purse strings as a general rule, allowed the entire sum of the funds to flow right through his fingers into the creation of a building in a Spanish-speaking country, nearly four thousand miles away from California in Central America. It made sense for him to be here. He is half Mexican, fluent in Spanish, happy to be sweaty in the tropics, living beyond all else to catch the perfect wave. For him, it made sense. For me? Not so much.

I wasn't forced into it because certainly I agreed, but *I couldn't have ever made this choice without him.* He was missioned with the endeavor. Steadfast. Blindly focused. We got the money and forty-eight hours before covid broke out in America, we signed a contract with a builder and made our first fifty-thousand-dollar payment.

As we were enjoying the wave of creation energy imagining what was possible with the land, the view, and the builder's vision, the rest of the world was getting sick and going into lockdown. We flew home to California from Costa Rica in early March of 2020. Our next visit back didn't happen for a year.

The next day, they closed the country.

We built the entire house on WhatsApp. Back and forth with the builder's, one hundred and one thousand decisions all made from the space of the imaginal realm. We did our best to envision what we couldn't see. To translate meters into inches. To pretend we were standing in the living room, the master bedroom, the California closet. It was an exercise in visual perception for sure.

And we fought.

We began noticing how differently we see the world. How we interact with our surroundings in such a different way. Me, a fast decision maker, quick to assimilate, trusting the divine plan that is unfolding around me, while at the same time trusting that the people doing the work know what they are doing. Him, careful. Calculated. Uncertain. Revisiting the choice again I thought we made yesterday. And again. And again. It would cause such anger and fury inside of me as I perceived we were wasting time while my perfectionist husband revisited things again and again. As I pushed for completion, things eroded. Things like self-esteem and self-confidence. I started to not like him, and he started to not like me. We were lost in the minutia completely overlooking the grand plan. Completely asleep to the brilliant orchestration by the universe.

I saw him as stingy and conservative. He saw me as extravagant and wasteful. We fell into a pattern of shaming each other back and forth for these characteristics. The more he squeezed, the more I spent. The more I spent, the more he shut down. This pattern would continue for a long while.

In January of 2021, we finally came back into Costa Rica. Arriving, for the first time, at the completed home site in the dark, which now flaunted a building that was brought into existence in obscured light. We'd never physically seen any of it live during creation. Tiptoeing around the perimeter of the house giggling, laughing, and filled with delight, we unwrapped our brand new, fully paid-for toy, under a bejeweled star-filled sky boasting the Milky Way.

We felt alive and connected.

The house is beautiful. It is pristine. All of it. The sleek modern open design allows in all the nature. The beautiful finishes of teak wood throughout make it complementary to the natural elements. We loved it and we loved being there. We saw it as a revenue opportunity. We found a property manager and rented the house. It was occupied nonstop for a year and a half.

The first women's retreat I decided to hold in Costa Rica sold out before I even marketed it. Almost overnight, it all came together. The location, the Spanish-speaking Canadian gal who is my "boots on the ground" coordinator for all activities, transportation, and details that need to be navigated in a foreign country. The location of unique individual Balinese-styled homes dotted throughout the property encircling Casa Grande where the main events took place. It all came together perfectly without a hitch. I mentioned it to a few women and voilà, it sold out. The retreat took place March of 2022, and it wasn't only my participants who experienced transformation.

In mid-April after being in the rainforest for six weeks, we descended into Los Angeles. The contrast of the rich, lush emerald jungle of Costa Rica was slammed with the concrete reality of hundreds of miles of cement as tinsel town came into view. I could feel the contraction of my spirit and the physical heaviness in my body as we came into the low-frequency, high-density reality of our home of twenty years.

From the window seat I looked over at Paul. In that split second without a word, the agreement was revealed to me through my inner knowing. It was as obvious as a sneeze coming on. To me, a clear insight. I felt like I was looking right at it. *The next phase of the soul contract was activated. In that moment, the magic elixir of our entelechy streamed through the crossroads finding the gateway onto the next path.*

I knew it as Truth inside myself, as sure as I was sitting crammed in a window seat on a hot airplane full of restless passengers impatiently waiting to charge the aisle. I felt the familiar flash of inner surety rise up in my chest and pass energy through the entirety of me. The overwhelming sensation of spirit rising within me.

I wasn't honest with him about the retreat.

I didn't fully disclose what happened there. I didn't share about how moved I was to witness Monique guiding my ladies through her acreage of trees, plants, flowers, herbs, shrubs, fruits, and cacao. A week before, I hadn't known what the hell cacao was, and the next day I would unknowingly serve it during a sound ceremony, but there I was sucking on a slimy covered seed with chalky chocolate powder breaking apart in my mouth as the butterflies danced around our heads. Petunia the pig grunted a big snort next to us, and Monique chattered on about the medicinal qualities of all the fragrant gifts she was sharing with us from her gardens.

I was enthralled. I was alive.

I didn't share with him that while I was facilitating during the retreat I received massive, unwelcomed, waves of clarity that *we are coming to live here*. Like the rude and abrupt shock of someone pushing their way through your front entry as you try and brace the door shut to keep them out.

Monique had something I continued to crave at a soul level. She had the Presence and the Essence of Being One with her environment. I recognized it and was being called to it. She stood as the picture of possibility as she floated from one moment to the next with no agenda, nowhere to get to, nothing more important than where she was right here and now. She walked over the earth barefoot, fearless about what anthill she may be disturbing or what creepy crawly might slither across her foot. She stood as the portraiture rendering the ease and simplicity of communing with the natural world and the elegance and beauty of how life can unfold. My soul was inspired and mesmerized by her. The pull was magnetic.

I didn't tell him how the waves of clarity came so loud and clear as they do and I felt terrified and panicked. See, I am *an indoor girl*. Playing in the dirt sounds sexy until there is crud under my nails and I'm fainting from the brutal heat. None of this makes any sense. But I knew during the retreat, and I knew right as the plane touched down at LAX, this was the next crazy move my soul was asking me to make. This was the next initiation. The next ask from God granting ascension to the higher levels. While I cognitively didn't have this clarity at the time, I also know I have no other option but to surrender to a plan that is not mine and to let God drive.

Trusting Yourself and the Plan for Your Life

This is the next gateway activating my entelechy, the fullest realized expression of who I came to *Be* in this life. This is another activation to the dynamic expression of my soul's code.

We all have this.

A dynamic code that is alive within the essence of our Being. I call it Original Wisdom, which is the inherent intelligence in all Beings rooted in unconditional love. All of us are powered with an essential program—think of it like software for a computer—that holds the literal map to realize the potential of who we came here to be in this life.

All souls must choose which path they will follow. There are multiple on ramps and exit ramps along the way. For me, I know I chose the path of the Spiritual Warrior. And, I know that is not a path for everyone.

Either way - you can't make a wrong move.

As far as your soul is concerned, it's literally impossible to take an off-target turn. All the turns, no matter what the path, invite our fullest expression. The bigger leaps—like marrying a guy you just met on the internet, enrolling yourself in a master's program in spiritual psychology on the advice of a psychic or stepping down from your twenty-eight-year highly successful, robustly tenured career and starting over in midlife—are activations.

Initiations of sort.

Not everyone has come to this life to awaken into the knowing that they are a Spiritual Being on an epic human adventure, but I definitely did. Not everyone will realize or recognize their True essence is comprised of the energy of Loving, but we are all the same whether you believe it or not. And, while it's a pretty bold claim to make, I am positive that the purpose of each of our lives is to blossom into the fullest expression of who we came here to be. And, because each of us really truly is made of love, realizing that Love inside of us is the grand intention of the journey.

The crazy courageous things we do in our life—the things that look illogical—the whims, the notions, the crazy impulses. These are the clues to a joy-filled and fully rich life. Saying yes to these soulful whims is answering the call to be transported to the next thruway that will unfold who you are and who you came here to be.

We are all asleep to our true magnificence.

Once a corporate robot, I invested my time, my energy, my precious life force and the oh-so-fucking-fleeting time we have here on this planet, hypnotized executing someone else's agenda. The corporation, the organization, the government, religion, ethnicities, your peer group, and even your own family wants you to fit into a perfect mold, behaving well-regulated, carrying out order and sensibility.

And, that is all part of it.

There is nothing wrong with any of it because it's all part of HOW we each wake ourselves up to discover we are so much more. All our souls, which hold this dynamic code, are able to activate the process of growth through a spiritual course of study. This is life's lesson plan. You've got one. I've got one. We've all got one. Some people will sail through their whole life without any interest or a clue about theirs. It's fine. It's all part of it. Not everyone is here to wake up.

But the people who are here, who are aware, who are under contract with their own Original Wisdom, are here to demonstrate what it looks like to be awake. And in so doing, they help awaken people who also came to this life to wake up. They hold the template energetically. And, I happen to believe (for a lot of Spiritual reasons I don't have the word count to list here) that globally, we have crossed the tipping point. Meaning, there is no turning back because humanity is destined to wake up.

Everyone is waking up. It's inevitable.

Further, because we all have an encrypted key guiding us toward our individual and collective full expression, *we can't get it wrong*.

So, what am I sharing here? What am I trying to say? Am I giving you a way to activate your code? Maybe, but not really.

See, your plan is your plan. There is nothing anyone can do to speed up their plan or enhance their plan or make their plan better or sweeter than anyone else's. *Your plan is between you and your Soul*. Between your Soul and the Great Divine Creator. The Universe. The Grand Overall Design. Your entire journey is about waking up to that!

Yet, what I do know from experience is that on the road to fulfillment, there are gateways and there are exit ramps. In 2016, I got a triple negative breast cancer diagnosis after dreaming I had a fish hook punctured through my left breast. By that time, I had a solid spiritual practice. I was meditating daily and listening for information and clues from my soul. (Hence the vivid dream.) Had I still been sleeping, perhaps I would have walked around a lot longer with a time bomb in my chest. This was an example of one of my built in exit plans. Instead of dying from an unbeatable cancer sentence, I learned how to love and support my sweet self. I learned about self-compassion, understanding, and deep radical acceptance.

To do that, I had to awaken. The cancer diagnosis was a gateway.

It was a road to access the higher part of me. The more aware part. The conscious part. It was a *right of entry* into the higher realms of conscious awareness, which in turn connect me to the next superhighway and the next and the next.

I have come to recognize that each gateway presents only *as I make the leap*. Quite literally, the gateway opens, *in the air*. Everyone wants to plan out their life and have all their stop gaps in place. Everyone feels secure when there is a nine-point plan with a timeline, a return on investment, and an exit strategy. We spend our whole lives trying to line up all these safety measures, and the only real thing that occurs when we make this our focus, is that we miss out on the rich dynamic adventure that is our life.

Not everyone will leap. Not everyone's Soul path is meant to. And, if you are meant to leap, *you will*. If you are meant to leap, that is why you are reading this right now. And as you leap, the gateway opens in the ethers. The way into the next level of your being, to ascend. If it helps, you can jump, bob, spring, prance, frolic, skip, or vault yourself because when you elevate, different options are presented. The options presented are completely different from anything that was available to you before the elevation. The options literally reveal themselves IN THE LEAP.

I categorize my leaps as high jumps. To many people, my vaulting crossovers look pretty crazy. This is not only how I continue to inspire my clients to make their own leaps, but it is most certainly part of the agreement I have with my soul waking myself up into higher, more exalted dimensional realms. All my moves are driven by Spiritual Ambition, my unrestrained desire to be awake on the planet today, as a self-honoring choice and the destiny of the dynamic self-propelling code within me.

So, here I am in Central America. In the rainforest of Costa Rica. The truth is, my soul knows exactly what I am doing here. My ego is just trying to catch up. Yet, I do have a few things to share about how to trust yourself and the plan for your life. If you want to know more, find my next book Spiritual Ambition.

About the Author

Donna Bond, M.A. is an Ignitor of Light, a spiritual life and business coach, author, and thought leader. Her mission as a soul-centered catalyst for personal transformation is to empower your Highest Self on your epic human adventure. After a twenty-eight-year run as a successful corporate marketing executive in hospitality who "had it all", she followed the lead of the Divine, entirely changed course in the middle of her life, and got a master's in spiritual psychology with an emphasis in consciousness, health and healing.

In her chapter, Donna reveals her firsthand experience of answering the next courageous call of her soul, activating the next phase of her personal evolution. Donna supports clients to live with reverence by activating their entelechy—the fullest realized expression of who they came here to be in this life. She guides her clients to do this from the inside out.

Donna is the author of the teaching memoir *Original Wisdom: Harness the Power of the Authentic You*. Original Wisdom is the inherent intelligence in all Beings rooted in unconditional love.

Donna and her husband, award-winning oil painter Paul Bond, moved full time to the rainforest of Costa Rica as her next courageous and illogical act of spiritual ambition, following the universe to where she was being led. Donna facilitates transformative, soul-centered one-to-one coaching, online group classes, and women's retreats.

Original Wisdom: Harness the Power of the Authentic You
https://donnabond.com/book/original-wisdom/
Website: www.donnabond.com
email: donna@donnabond.com

- instagram.com/donnabondcoach
- linkedin.com/in/donnabond
- youtube.com/@donnabond

TWO

Stacie Cooper

REBIRTH INTO MOTHERHOOD

The "shoulds" in our lives are stifling. My most stifling motherhood shoulds were how the birth of my son *should* go, how my postpartum recovery *should* be, and how I *should* seamlessly fall into this new role, this new balancing act of countless identities and responsibilities with grace and ease. This chapter is a glimpse into the beginning of this beautiful yet challenging season wrought with whys, why nots, why me's, and why can't I's—but more importantly, my rebirth as a mother, an identity I never envisioned for my life. It is a glimpse into the shoulds I encountered during my unexpectedly traumatic delivery, the loneliness and loss and pain and shame of early postpartum, and my awkward stumbling into balancing new roles, integrating new parts of myself, and reconnecting with my hummingbird, my heart, my feminine power, and myself.

***

Control. Is. An. Illusion. The plan was to have a plan…and then to let go of attachment to the plan. I wanted a "natural" birth. I had watched countless how-to YouTube videos to prepare: how to breathe, how to stay calm, how to avoid medication, how to use hypnobirthing,

birthing balls, birthing tubs, birthing playlists…you name it. I convinced myself: *I got this! I teach mindfulness and meditation.*

But I was forcing masculine expectations onto the profoundly feminine experience of entering into motherhood. The second I walked in for my thirty-nine-week check-up, I had to scrap my plan. *All* twenty bullet points on my beautifully designed birth plan—typed in ten-point font—were canceled out, one by one, over the course of a grueling, painful, gut-wrenching, heart-wrenching, soul-wrenching week in the hospital.

It all started on a regular day with a regular prenatal check-up and a blood pressure (BP) cuff. I'd always considered myself pretty damn healthy. Pilates, yoga, hikes, bikes, green smoothies, meditation, plenty of time outside. Every time I went in for a visit with my midwives, it was quick, uneventful, and they'd comment on how I was healthier than most of their much-younger patients. I was proud, prideful, not gonna lie. Until this visit…the BP monitor started beeping obnoxiously. The nurse awkwardly muttered something under her breath, scurrying out of the room. The midwife entered moments later, trying to act calm—I could see it in her eyes. "Your BP is abnormally high; we need to run it again. It's probably a fluke. Keep your arm down, relax, breathe."

Like the good student I'd always been, I followed along, practicing my meditation mantra in my head as I breathed slowly, citing research in my head proving this could *control* my physical experience. It didn't work. The machine kept beeping loudly and incessantly, like an alarm every time the cuff released its air and released its grip on my arm. I felt like a failure to my profession: I was sent down the hall for more labs.

I went home and, again, watched YouTube videos on preparing for natural childbirth.

Ring ring.

"Come back in, we need to do more tests. Don't worry, it shouldn't take long."

I drove up, sure I'd get home in time to keep my afternoon Pilates session. Again, feeling like I had some semblance of control over my "plan."

I checked in. They led me back to the triage area and gave me a scratchy hospital gown. I was confused. I asked the nurse if I'd be out in time for Pilates. She took my BP and gave me a look I'll never forget: a sincere mix of pity and concern. "The midwife will come back to discuss your results."

After fifteen excruciatingly long minutes, she entered, inhaled deeply, and sat down next to me. "I think it's time we call your husband."

Uh oh.

I don't remember the details of the conversation—only a few keywords: "preeclampsia," "alarmingly high values," and "Immediate. Emergency. Medical. Induction." The polar opposite of what I wanted: Natural. Non-invasive. Labor...*Shit*. There go the first three bullet points on my birth plan. Control...failed. Expectations...sabotaged.

Scramble. Make the calls.

Who is watching our dog...packing our bags?!

"I'm going to walk outside while we wait for my husband."

"No, sorry. Your BP is severely high; you are high risk for seizures—we can't let you walk around unsupervised."

"Can I at least get checked into my fancy birthing suite and take a bath?"

"No, I'm sorry. You're high risk...you can no longer be admitted to the suites."

No birthing ball, no tub, no nice room with a big bed and a view.

Standard hospital room it is. *Ugh*.

Well, at least there's no IV—that was my main priority.

"I'm sorry, we need to hook you up to a magnesium drip…STAT. It's standard practice for preeclampsia."

What does that mean?

BEDRIDDEN. Unable to get up and move. Tubes coming out of both arms. No privacy. Constantly being monitored. Poked and prodded hourly, day and night. My worst nightmare.

One more item "Xed" off the plan. And another. And another.

The second my husband shows up, they're ready to start. The sense of urgency among the medical staff is palpable. They tell me the plan: Medicate and dilate.

I detest medications. They recommend two right off the bat: Cytotec to get things "softened and opening" and Pitocin, on a steadily increasing dose, to "ease" my body into unnatural, premature labor. Two things I had vehemently opposed.

The female body is not meant to dilate and open when it's not ready.

They want to start with the "least invasive" option: A Foley catheter bulb.

"What is that?"

"We insert and inflate it like a balloon. It helps encourage a 'gentle' opening."

Gentle my ass. They put the bed flat (which, having a large, pregnant belly, can quickly make you feel dizzy or pass out), lock my feet in stirrups, tell me to let my knees fall out to the sides, and "relax."

She shoves a rubber tube up. Ouch. I've been to the OB/GYN many times, but this was significantly more painful.

"Sorry, you're not dilated enough. We'll give it another try."

She shoves the tube up…and again. I feel sweat pouring out my pores. I get shaky, clammy, nauseous.

My husband is holding my hand, telling me to keep looking at him and breathe. I have no clue WTF is going on around me. I hear a lot of beeps, people mumbling anxiously.

Everything. Goes. Dark.

A few minutes later, I'm shaking uncontrollably. The midwife is standing next to me. She looks embarrassed. The mag hit me too hard…that combined with being on my back for too long, nine months pregnant, and having a huge rubber tube shoved up my too-tight cervix had sent my heart into shock. A crash cart and six hospital staff had immediately rushed in after my heart almost stopped…and…my baby's.

They would give me a break to rest.

Ding ding ding. Next round. Try again.

Shove the tube. No success.

Pump more meds. No success.

My body does not like being forced to open when it isn't ready. It's happened once before….

Tears stream down my face, clenched fists, *I can do this.*

It works. Fourth time's a charm.

Increase the Pitocin. *Drip drip drip.*

Now, we wait for things to progress.

It's been over twenty-four hours…

"Can I eat? I'm starving."

"No, sorry."

"Can I drink? I'm so thirsty."

"No, sorry."

"Can I walk around?"

"No, sorry."

Ten. Hours. Later.

Thousands. Of. Contractions. Later.

"You're just not progressing as we'd hoped. We're so sorry."

Doctors enter. Carrying metal chairs. Place them around me in a circle. *Clink clank.* Somber tone.

"We need to discuss pain management options."

"We're so sorry."

"We know you wanted a natural birth."

"You're just not progressing."

It's. Been. So. Long.

I'm exhausted.

"It's been so long. You're exhausted."

Sigh.

Defeated.

"Yes, yes, fine. Whatever you recommend."

Dr. Feelgood enters.

He does it quickly. Icy cold sharp pain in my back. Tears stream down my face. I try to hide it. *Be strong. Millions of women before me have done this. I am not alone.*

"This will help you take the edge off. And sleep. You need rest to keep going."

Everything starts to fade....

"It's time to try again," the nurse says.

Increase the Pitocin. Again.

Drip drip drip.

Now, we wait for things to progress. Again.

"We know you said no breaking your water unnaturally, but it would really help you progress."

Stirrups. Spread legs. They break my water with what looks like a long crochet needle.

Thank God for the epidural. I can barely feel anything.

The contractions start again.

More Xes off the birth plan. Stirrups. Spread legs. Shove the internal monitor up and tape it to my leg. Shove a catheter in and tape it to my other leg.

So many tubes. So much tape. So many needles. So many places.

So many things being monitored…my heartbeat. My baby's heartbeat. My BP. My blood. My uterus.

I feel like all my modesty and freewill are gone. This is supposed to be a beautiful and sacred experience, not controlled, cold, clinical.

Increase the Pitocin. Again.

Drip drip drip.

Now, we wait for things to progress. Again.

Hours. Later.

"We're so sorry. You're just not progressing."

I already know what's going to happen. My worst nightmare…being cut open. Awake.

The rest is a blur.

Wheeling on a bed down the hall, fluorescent lights fly by overhead. Entering a bright, cold, sterile room surrounded by faceless people masked in scrubs. Somber tone.

"You will feel a cool liquid entering your spine."

"Let me know if you can feel your chest." No, nothing….

"Your toes?" No, nothing….

"Good."

Familiar faces at my head. A curtain over my chest so I can't see below.

It goes so fast. My husband is holding my hand, showing me pictures of my dog to distract me.

Seconds later, I hear a scream.

"Do you want to see your baby?"

Dr. Feelgood holds up a mirror.

All I see are my bloody guts split open on the table.

"Umm, can you please move the mirror?"

There he is…I see my baby.

He is healthy, they say!

A wave of relief.

I start shaking uncontrollably. Violent tremors. Violent chills.

They bring my baby to my chest and put him on me. He is shaking. I am shaking.

We slow down…we stop shaking. Together. Our heartbeats sync. I never imagined myself as a mother, but in that moment my heart cracked open and I became his.

The rest of the *long* week in the hospital is a blur.

Bright lights.

Screaming baby.

Needles shoved in.

Blood drawn out.

No humility.

Nurses grabbing my boobs.

"Here is how you breastfeed," they demonstrate.

Beep, beep beep!

"Your BP is too high."

"You can't go home."

"You can't go outside."

Sobbing, despairing, in pain.

Just. Let. Me. Go. Home.

Finally. Cleared to go home. For reals.

Adios, muthafuckas.

We. Go. Home.

As a family.

Deep breath. *Deeper* sigh of relief. We survived. I survived.

This is my birth story. I read tons of birth stories before giving birth, but only the shiny, happy ones where things went seamlessly. I avoided the messy ones...the stories of perils, pains, setbacks, surgeries, traumas, and tragedies. I am a doctor of clinical psychology. I work with teens through a lens of strengths and mindfulness. I am a control freak. I am type A. I am used to getting As and succeeding at everything I do. So how did I approach preparing for labor and motherhood? What did I do? What I do best...I prepared. I planned. I thought I could plan and control the outcome by putting on blinders to the things that could go wrong. If I programmed my mind and used my training to visualize the outcome, I could ensure a positive, blissful experience.

The next part of my story is of the less-talked-about enigmatic period…the postpartum period—to unearth and bring to light not the beauty that comes from entering into parenthood and reaching a new level of unconditional love, but the perils of *my* postpartum period: the nitty gritty, messy, lonely, shameful, rageful, painful, triggering, terrifying parts, and my rebirthing as a mother.

The weekly prenatal checkups and check-ins dissolve into the ether once the baby is on the outside. Where do the support and resources go after parents are handed their baby and leave the hospital? This is a time when I believe they're needed the most. Reassurance, encouragement, basic resources, basic help, validation, normalization, information…all I got was a pamphlet on postpartum depression and an offer to call the doctor "if needed." During my pregnancy and delivery, I felt like a bug under a microscope. As soon as I left the hospital, in a wheelchair, unable to barely move or take care of my own basic needs, questioning my sanity many times, with a perfect little human being to care for nonetheless, I felt like a ship lost out at sea during a storm at night with no compass, no radio, no lights, no one to guide me safely to shore.

My story is neither new nor unique. My goal is to help new moms, especially older and professional moms like me who are grappling with how to recover, receive help, and accept this new role, feel like they are not alone, are not crazy, and are doing their best. No one can ever truly prepare you for parenthood. Even if new moms say they're "doing great, aside from little sleep," I know firsthand there's so much more to the story. It's a beautiful time, of course, but it can also be one of the most physically and emotionally taxing times for many new mothers. Hormonal shifts are *extreme* and sent me on an emotional roller coaster daily. There's a lot of shame around admitting this and stigma around asking for help or complaining.

So what do I remember in the aftermath of coming home? Feeling scared and unprepared. Feeling helpless and useless, immobile in my bed. Feeling angry and ashamed with myself as a woman who wasn't "doing it all," "doing it right," or "doing enough."

I have mad respect for people who do it alone. I can't imagine. I barely hung on by a frayed thread *with* support. I never had experience with babies—I came into this flying blind. I never had a "motherly instinct" or felt my "biological clock ticking." I was afraid to hold babies, worried I would break them. And I prepared myself for a natural birth and recovery, not preeclampsia and an emergency Cesarean. I accepted physical support and emotional nurturance from my husband and our doula, who had such a nurturing and nonjudgmental nature, exactly what I needed in my darkest moments of the early postpartum fog. Their love and help allowed me to remember how to nurture and mother myself once this season had passed.

What else do I remember in those initial hazy weeks? Feeling ashamed of my annoyance when well-meaning loved ones came to visit to meet our baby. It felt insurmountable and overwhelming to have the energy to get up to greet them. My innate need to be a polite and gracious hostess was hard to bypass and ignore. However, our baby constantly slept or ate or cried or peed or pooped, so any planned visit was stressful since it interrupted one of these and my *desperate* need for rest and a moment of peace in a crazy household with crazy hormones. I was mad at myself for being irritated, since I appreciated their love and support dearly, and for having a hard time saying no out of guilt. Simple "How are you doing/what do you need?" texts were most appreciated, and one girlfriend had a delicious four-course meal dropped at our doorstep: it was our first real dinner in over a week.

Oh, and my twelve-year-old dog Toby, my first child, was largely forgotten. This was hard on me (and him, I'm sure, as he could barely walk due to hip dysplasia and bad arthritis). Usually showered with love and affection, Toby quietly, patiently, sat by and waited for us to feed him and take him out a few times a day. I had to muster my almost-nonexistent energy to keep myself awake and functioning and serve as a cow supplying milk for my hungry little guy.

All in all, I feel like I went in clueless to this whole motherhood experience. The first few months, I continued to feel ill-equipped, relying on those I trusted to guide me through the foggy, mucky, messy mess. At times I crawled and clawed my way through. Never have I felt such a wave of hormonal ups and downs, such despair, such rage, such a sense of helplessness and hopelessness the week I had to quit breastfeeding cold-turkey and simultaneously say goodbye to my fur child and best bud, Toby. Later, I learned about how extreme hormonal changes are when you quit breastfeeding *gradually*, much less overnight, as I was forced to do the *same week* Toby took his last breath in my arms in our backyard. In my darkest moments, I found myself curled in a ball on the floor of my closet—hopeless, lost, angry at myself, screaming, feeling like my family would be better off without me, wondering how I would go on, and why I was "so emotional."

But I did survive. I learned hard lessons of humility and resilience through the process. I learned to ask for help, as I had no choice at times. I learned to set boundaries for the first time in my forty years on this planet. And often the boundaries I set were my mama bear way of protecting this new little precious boy who captured my heart.

Somewhere in the haze of madness, crying, pain, loneliness, fear, and anger at myself for not "doing it better," I reconnected with my inner hummingbird, my feminine archetype, the messenger of love and connection. Tapping into my hummingbird through movement, connection, and spending time in nature grounded and balanced me. Yoga, Reiki, Pilates, sweating it out in spin, walks, sharing emotions with friends, crying, screaming, laughing, writing this…whatever it takes. I've since been trying to share my experience, be open with my struggles, and move that energy through me in as many ways I can think of so I can feel like myself again, or a new-and-improved version of myself, and be better for those I love. I also reframed my femininity, my hummingbird, and my highly sensitive and emotional nature as superpowers that allow me to connect to myself, others, and life on a profound level. Most importantly, learning to mother myself allowed me to fully embrace and flourish in my new role as a mother.

I don't think there is one right way to enter motherhood, but I do believe withholding and hiding and isolating are harmful. So my only parting advice is, do what *you* need to do to move energy through you and remind yourself you are STRONGER than you think. Mother yourself, nurture yourself as you would a dear friend…or your own child. Be easy on yourself. Seek out support from those who have been through it or with whom you feel safe, loved, and validated. You are not alone. You are not crazy. You are doing your best. And everything, everywhere is love.

About the Author

Dr. Stacie Cooper is a published author, transition coach, and Pilates and mindfulness instructor with twenty years of experience helping teens and young adults on their journey to uncover their strengths, find purpose, and navigate major life transitions. In 2009, she graduated from Pepperdine University with her doctorate in clinical psychology and completed her training at Duke University's student counseling center.

Stacie has had a passion for working with teens and women in transition for her entire career and founded Aware and Thriving in 2016 to focus on preventative and strengths-based efforts emphasizing mind and body. She has been a mentor for Girls Incorporated's College Bound Mentorship Program and a keynote speaker for their Eureka summer camp for middle school girls. She teaches group reformer Pilates classes in the local community and private reformer sessions out of her house.

Stacie started writing as a child and is now excited to be pursuing this passion more formally. She first published a fiction novel, *The Masks We Wear*, in 2012 and more recently, two self-help workbooks for teens with New Harbinger, first on self-harm and then on trauma and adversity. She got married and had a baby boy in 2021, which has inspired her to venture into the world of picture books, her first one being a playful rhyming book encouraging children to find creative ways to stay active and play outdoors.

She currently lives in San Juan Capistrano, California, with her husband, baby boy, and Golden Retriever.

Website: www.awareandthriving.com

instagram.com/stacielcooper
linkedin.com/in/stacie-cooper-57578922

THREE

Danielle Dawson

FINDING THE MISSINGNESS: SHAME AS A GATEWAY
TO DEEP LOVE AND CONNECTION

Something Missing

At around the end of 2016, perhaps twelve months after having my second child, I was sitting in the lounge room of my Sydney apartment with my two baby boys. At home, I would often struggle to sit, play, and be present with them and would often find myself not really with them. In sharing what I'm about to share, I can't really say it's a memory but more of a shift in my state of being. I remember this kind of hovering, taking a bird's-eye view of the scene below me, which saw me separate from my babies. It was like I was in a protective bubble or a world of my own.

As a young girl, I'd always wanted to be a mother, and I wanted to be a brilliant one at that. One where my kids would yell out to me, " You're the best mummy in the world!" During pregnancy, I read many parenting advice books so as to make sure I was cut out to do the job properly. I had feared that as a new parent, I may be judged or reprimanded where I got it wrong, and so the books acted as a buffer of protection for me. If anyone was going to tell me I was doing it wrong,

I could say, well, this is how they said to do it in these books. I implemented that therein, and my baby boys responded perfectly.

To the outside world, it looked like I had it all together and that I was doing all the right things as a first-time parent. My babies were the perfect textbook babies, and I had strived for it. As I would watch all the other happy mums and passersby in the streets, I told myself that my life was doomed to fail because, on the inside, I felt sad and alone. When at home by ourselves, I really struggled to play and connect with my boys, but I wanted so badly to have something deeper in connection with myself and with them. I would always have the intention of making time to sit with them, but then I would become distracted in the unconscious patterns of finding something else to do that I told myself was more important. The inner voice of shame would ridicule me for not giving them more of me. *You can't even sit and play with your kids for five minutes. What's five minutes? Do you seriously think you're a good mum?* And then the feelings of guilt and shame would leave my whole body feeling numb and disconnected. I was in a paradox – so desperately wanting to be present with my kids yet disconnected when I had the opportunity.

Throughout my life, I'd never really heard anyone speak about feeling a sense of missingness or incompleteness within themselves, so, I thought it was just me and that there was something wrong with me. The more I started to speak with others through my professional training, the more I understood that the missingness I felt was real amongst many. I believe every single soul comes into this world with a desire to feel deep love and connection, and that it is something innate in each and every one of us. Where childhood circumstances were not able to nurture this desire within, it leaves us with this sense that something is incomplete. And so the journey back to wholeness is one that we as our adult selves are able to nurture for our child within.

Doing As A Means To Finding Wholeness

For years, an unconscious pattern had been playing inside of me; in childhood, in school, in my career, in my love life: if you do this, then you will feel the completeness you are looking for;   or if only you do that, then you'll have it. I'd try to be the perfect partner, daughter, colleague, employee, sister, wife, income earner, student, business owner, mother…   the list kept going. I twisted myself into a perfectionistic multi-tasking pretzel, with the unconscious belief that the missingness was something someone outside of me could give to me.

In 2014 my first son was brought into the world by planned C-section. Holding him in my arms for the first time was the most precious joyful gift of my life. I was flooded with feelings of peace, love, and joy. After surgery, I remember returning to a private room in the hospital where a realisation came to me and my energy state completely shifted from one of joy, love, and peace to one where I felt panic, guilt, and shame. I knew at a subconscious level that having a child wasn't the answer to finding the missingness I was looking for. I felt hurt and heartbroken, I'd been telling myself these stories for years as to where I'd find this missingness, and still, I hadn't found it. My emotional walls went from being down, open, and receptive to love, to one of my walls going straight back up and being emotionally closed off.

With the realisation that I played the persona of the good girl most of my life, I'm sad to say but not regretful of the lessons, that I was a younger unhealed part of me. I was the people pleaser, the girl scared to say no, the girl who didn't ask questions or say how she felt and what she needed – because that would have been too selfish of her, and most definitely there was no standing up for what she believed in what was true to her – that would have created a situation of conflict or confrontation and she'd be to blame. With the deepest empathy for my younger self, she'd learnt a false dynamic that set her up for failure in all relationships. From a young age, she had learnt to self-sabotage to keep safe, and it continued in all my relationships until eventually, I started to wake up. To paraphrase Rumi, I was being cleared out for some new delight.

Inner Work

Over the last six years through therapy, coaching, and an intense pull in the direction of self-learning and self-discovery, I have been peeling back the layers and discovering the truth of who I am; one discovery is that I am an empath (someone who feels the emotional state of others). From as young as I can remember, I have always been able to feel others' emotions deeply and so as I would talk with or be around others I would unconsciously merge and match their inner emotional state, however, what I didn't realise was that not everyone does this. As an unskilled empath, it was my normal – and as I understand it now, being highly sensitive is that of a sensitive nervous system – a trait you're born with. People had always said things to me like *wow I don't know what it is about you but you're so lovely*. I would feel a sense of pride, that in some way others weren't able to offer what I offered at an emotional level, and as an unquestioned belief, I guess I just thought I was really good at being there for people more than others.

Being able to discern whose feelings belong to who, and not allowing myself to stay in another's emotional state beyond that which is necessary, has been key for me not only in understanding who I am at my core but in helping myself and others to regulate their own emotions. Learning to know and understand myself has also helped me to develop a deep sense of self-worth, self-love, self-trust, self-respect, self-confidence, and self-compassion for myself.

When empaths learn emotional discernment, they learn a brilliant skill to be able to truly empathise with others and separate themselves from the emotion of the other —however, when it's unconscious it can contribute to situations that can quickly become toxic. In having a safe and trusted space to talk with my coaches and mentors, as well as practices such as meditation and yoga, I was able to question limiting thoughts and old beliefs, as well as quiet the mind and body to let go of the old and make space for the new. From this place, I operate my life from a more conscious space of living which in turn allows the natural process of change, growth, and evolution to evolve through me.

The journey of awakening meant playing with the idea that my very existence was larger than my small self – that there was a larger force happening in the universe in which we live. I had no idea what that meant for me. At the time I thought, *I don't want to go to church, I don't know how to meditate,* and I had negative judgments about yoga. However, what I later realised was that I was unconsciously already on the path of finding something spiritual in my life. My boys were attending a Montessori school, as I was passionate about the teaching philosophy being grounded in spiritual principles, and I'd signed up to do a Diploma in Montessori Education. I hadn't yet linked that my passion for my boys' spiritual education was, in fact, part of the germination process for my deepest desire to wholeness being fulfilled.

As I understand it now, everything in life happens to us so as to get us back on track to becoming whole and truly ourselves. When we have the bravery and courage to look inwards and go deep, we create safety, trust, self-love, and self-acceptance in ourselves like never before. This then means we are able to create the secure relationships we truly desire, where we can be vulnerable and connect to our innermost feelings, needs, beliefs, and desires so that we can have the deep love, connection, and emotional intimacy we so longingly desire for ourselves and for those we are in relationship with. As I continue to grow and learn more about the truth of who I am, I pick up that my boys' internal worlds are also changing. I sense they too are becoming more aware of their feelings, needs, and desires as well as feeling empowered to express themselves in a way they never have before.

Self-Discovery

In 2021, I enrolled myself in an online course related to non-violent communication as I was trying to find better ways to communicate. I knew in my heart of hearts that my communication skills were holding me back both in relationships and in my self-confidence to do something larger within my community. One particular module on that course was life-changing for me, and it connected me to a part of me that had long been lost.

Inner Critic work was something I had come across before, however, this time something significant happened. In this particular practice, we met our inner critic and understood what it looked like and how it talked to us. My inner critic is a younger, not-so-nice me—I feel she reflects my dark side, my shadows (the parts I never liked to admit I had). She is eight or nine years old, and she likes to laugh a cackling laugh at me whilst immersing herself in a steamy shower. In hindsight, she's the one with anger, rage, jealousy, and who is selfish - the unexpressed mean girl so as to not get into trouble and risk not getting the love she so anxiously yearned for. For others, the inner critic can be an animal, a figure of their imagination, their mother, their father.

My spiritual teacher had mentioned in our course that when we go deep with the inner critic, it often has an absolute treasure for us. The logical part of my mind couldn't quite comprehend this, but this time I truly trusted in my heart that there was a higher guidance about to support me and so I delved in to find my treasure.

The voice of the inner critic is the voice of shame; the one that tells me I'm not good enough, that I need to do better, and that there's something wrong with me. So the purpose of the exercise was to sit or imagine sitting on the ground with two cushions. Sitting on one cushion you would bring forth the voice of the critic and then moving onto the other cushion you would bring forth a softer, more loving, and caring voice. The kind voice would gently create a dialogue with the fierce voice and ask it to be kind and gentle.

For this exercise, I started by looking at my life history as a timeline of events and thought, *which of these have I thought about and gone into time and time again and which ones have I not?* As I traveled through the timeline, I got to a certain event that was glossed over as "sex with x". The dialogue between my inner critic and the gentle kind loving voice was truly beautiful to experience. But to cut it short, the meaning my younger self had stamped on this particular event in my timeline of glossy…was in fact not glossy at all. She'd put a shiny layer on top of a dull layer to mask the shame she felt so badly, and it needed to be broken down.

The event in mention had happened when I was around eighteen years old. Whilst out on a night out with friends, a known male - twice my age would pass me a glass of wine every time my glass was almost empty. In going in to meet my eighteen-year-old self, I knew that insecurity was her nature, and she lacked confidence and authority. These traits meant that the male attention she was receiving boosted her self-esteem and she secretly felt seen by a man who turned out to be a sexual predator. At my core, my intuition whispered it was wrong to accept the drinks, but the good girl persona was embedded so deeply that it became who I was - I didn't have access to my fierce shadows to the *no thank you, leave me alone*. That would have been rude and obnoxious and I would have hurt someone else's feelings. So I politely accepted the drinks as they kept coming. On waking up the morning after, my eighteen-year-old self had no recollection of leaving the bar or how she'd made her way to her hotel room with this man who now lay in the bed beside her. She said the worst part of this story was that the next morning when she woke, this man rolled on top of her to penetrate her, and she didn't say no, she said she had no voice, that it was frozen. She described her body as just there, like that of a corpse.

In witnessing my inner child's pain from a place of highest guidance with love, truth, and compassion, the shame trapped inside my body began to release with the significant throbbing of my throat and shaking of my body. This was the moment it dawned on me that I'd suppressed my voice most of my life and that somewhere, somehow I had learnt as a young child that I wasn't worthy to have a voice. What came to my awareness in writing this chapter, was that every single thing in my life had been leading me to this exact knowing - that there was a voice inside of me, unexpressed, unheard, and not living from her truth. In finding my voice, my whole world was about to change.

Every good girl has shadows that are yearning to come forth; selfishness, competitiveness, authoritativeness, neediness as well being the victim and the perpetrator. All aspects of humanity serve a purpose, and all are healthy energies at times. In Western society, young girls are told *to be good, do as they are told, listen to and respect their elders....* This then often results in them not listening to themselves, their inner knowing, their intuition and it creates little girls who disconnect from the truth of who they are. As women, we are also told "you create your own reality, and therefore you must take on the responsibility for your own actions." I myself had this subconscious belief, and by having it, I had weakened myself, and I made it okay that someone had done harm to me. Where women can accept that sometimes they are victims, they can acknowledge not everything is their fault. My truth was that I had taken on someone else's indiscretion and made it my fault. We are not here to be all good; we were each given the gift of dark shadows because they are what make us whole. When used in combination with love, dark shadows help us to create healthy boundaries for ourselves and others. The perpetrator, the one that does harm to others, is both healthy and unhealthy. This man, however, had extremely unhealthy amounts of this dark shadow, and I too had unhealthy amounts—I was lacking.

Wholeness

The journey to wholeness is one on which we are all inevitably being guided. Where we have the courage to go within, question limiting thoughts and beliefs, and surrender to the pain of our past, we can connect to the truth of who we are and begin to integrate all fragmented parts of us. Where we create safety, trust, and acceptance from within we can create secure foundations for healthy relationships with ourselves and with others. From here we get to become the most grounded, authentic version of ourselves, and the changemakers we came here to be.

About the Author

Where women lead from their deepest truth, they are doing the real work of restoring equilibrium in the world

Danielle Dawson is a qualified life coach and qualified transformational leader. She was the founder and director of Sydney and Country Mortgages, a home loan and commercial lending provider, before leaving to fulfill her dreams of self-transformation, writing, and coaching.

In her chapter, Danielle reveals how she felt something was missing in her life and the places she went to find it. She shares how bringing awareness to unconscious thoughts and beliefs helped her to connect to the deeper truth of who she is. In sharing her story, she hopes that other women will feel supported in their journey of growth, so that they to can know there is meaning behind the suffering, and that they are not alone in their journey.

As a coach, Danielle helps intelligent professional women bring forth and connect to all aspects of who they are on their path of self-actualization. Through her coaching, she supports women to connect to the deeper truth of who they are, and to create the healthy secure relationships they so longingly desire in their lives.

Danielle is a contributing author to the book *The Queen Bee: Embody Your Truth & Live Fully Expressed.*

Danielle received her professional coach certification and transformational leader certification from The Institute of Woman-Centered

Coaching, Training and Leadership. She holds certification in interpersonal neurobiology – attachment and relational resilience across the lifespan from The Mindsight Institute. She has a diploma in finance from Kaplan Professional, Sydney, Australia, and has over fifteen years of international banking experience in wealth management.

Website: danielledawson.com.au
Email: hello@danielledawson.com.au

instagram.com/danielledawson_coaching
linkedin.com/in/danielledawsoncoaching

FOUR

Carol DeFrancisco

FINDING YOUR BEAUTY

*B*eauty is within all of us. We all have internal and external beauty. The beauty inside us, feeds and enhances our external beauty. This is a journey to find the beauty within ourselves.

> Beautifulness is our birthright.

> *"Beauty begins when you become who you really are."*
> —Coco Chanel

Whether found in nature, in the arts or within ourselves, beauty is wild, magical and undefinable. Though not easily defined, this divine quality is deeply felt; it soothes us, opens our hearts and stirs powerful sensations of pleasure.

Beauty is so important because it connects us to our spirit. This connection with spirit opens a portal to a realm of unimaginable power and love.

Beauty is powerful. One small example; Stendhal syndrome is a term given to the phenomenon of observing art and being overwhelmed by the beauty being observed. People have been known to faint and go weak in the knees from ecstasy. I've had the experience myself while viewing paintings from the renaissance at the Uffizi in Florence and the Louvre in Paris. I remember my disbelief at the penetrating exquisiteness of the images before me; I was unable to contain within my body the power of such beauty. I had to find a place to sit down. Power, manifesting as personal empowerment is one of the many benefits of owning and embodying your beauty.

We are all keepers of beauty. Sometimes, in our culture, we have been trained to see beauty as 'other', that is, other than us. We are bombarded with images from a glamour cult; pictures of simulated perfection which seem to be saying, "This is what beauty looks like." When beauty is defined by externals we are caged in by an image of glamour that has a hard edge. These constructs are external to ourselves, and are defined by persons and systems which have nothing to do with the essence of who we truly are.

Not only are we told what beauty is, it's implied that we ourselves may or may not be acceptable let alone beautiful. We may be not beautiful enough or worse, we are too beautiful, too sexy, too curvy, attracting too much attention; or too plain, too thin, too big, too small, too much and also not enough. Or sometimes all of the above. Compared to what? Compared to an artificial, mechanical creation which seeks control with the message "You are not good enough."

Who has been left in charge of quantifying, and judging our beauty? The realm of this important matter must not be left in the hands of antiquated self-appointed patrons. Why would we give to an outer source the power to decide for us if we have beauty or not? Yet, we have found ourselves enmeshed in this quagmire; that is, allowing comparison to diminish our sense of self.

Haven't we all enjoyed the loveliness of a creature or a part of nature that appeared to be less than perfect but has filled us with wonderment? Nature produces beauty in abundance. Who is to say that the color of an iris is diminished by golden sunsets. Can we extend the same grace and lack of judgment to our own selves, our bodies, our beings?

"Beauty begins when you become who you truly are" because in the becoming, masks and armoring are removed. With these barriers dissolved, your inner radiance is revealed. Becoming beautiful does not have so much to do with adding things or changing one's physicality but with removing the obstacles to seeing clearly and to being clearly seen. Masks of fear, insecurity, comparison, and feelings of not measuring up can obscure the very essence of which our beauty is composed.

Beauty is healing. In discovering our beauty, we unwrap the layers that have prevented us from being seen and from emanating this quality to others and to the world. The masks and armoring that we have used for protection and denial create a fog around us. It is as if we have been carrying a lantern but only now have turned it on. The quality of light that emanates from us as we own our beauty is turned up and contains nuance that wasn't there before. This light is deeply healing having the capacity to mend our wounds, our sadness and loneliness and to obliterate the lies that we have told ourselves and have accepted from others.

As we unleash and radiate our truest quality, our beauty, we can be seen.

In our most secret moments, we long for or even suspect that we may have beauty of our own even if our personal attributes seem to pale in comparison to the iconic celebrity. We can transmute the lack or shame that we may experience in "coming up short" into our very own super power.

Pursuing our beauty as a super power is far from superficial. The appearance of beauty coalesces and forms around an interior sense of who we are, our light. Pleasantness of appearance is amplified by the qualities that are inside of us.

In other words, discovering and embodying your most core strength, attribute, gift or characteristic enhances your physical appearance. It is often hard to see this particular distinguishing quality within; it is your nature therefore can be difficult to notice. It is something inherent within you. It is your beauty, your super power.

When you know yourself as beautiful everything will change for you.

"You are beautiful just the way you are, and when you perceive your own beauty your emotional reaction is a reaction of love."
—Don Miguel Ruiz

We are not separate from the beauty that we seek. We all have beauty, we reveal it or mask it; often, the masking is simply our own denial. When we find our beauty and acknowledge it, we can embody it.

Embodiment is the ability to go beyond the mind to consciously bring our core beauty into our physical body. To hold it, contain it, strengthening and regenerating ourselves.

Upon discovering our sacred beauty, we can begin the practice of embodiment. We do this by breathing this quality into our heart center, and then dropping it into our belly, just below the navel into the sacral chakra. This is the place in our body which rules creation and attraction and is often represented by the butterfly. Butterfly totem is the signature for this space in the body because of the butterfly shaped hip bones which form our sacral bowl and because of the powerful transformation that happens to a butterfly as it emerges from its cocoon.

The sacral chakra is the seat of transformation; it becomes a chalice performing the alchemy of transmutation. It holds our dreams and creations and cradles the womb space where, gender aside, our creations are seeded and nurtured. The sacral chakra holds the energy of birth and manifestation.

Embodying our gift, our true beauty, helps us to attract and then manifest our desires in a more consistent manner; the desires of our soul becoming organized around a unified thought-form or center. Formlessness becomes form congealing around the center of our power.

We begin walking in our power.

You begin walking in your power.

To find and then embody your beauty, you must release the chatter of the ego mind. (I call this chattering ego mind "the beast.") The beast steals our energy with its anxiety and criticism. This beast does not speak the wisdom of our true inner being but can sound very real and loud. Because the beast feeds on our negative emotions, it knows our triggers and all of our weak points. It is consistent and persistent. This beast stands guard over the buried treasure within us and uses distraction and fear to throw us off the trail of this treasure within.

To uncover our buried treasure we must dispose of the layers of lies that we have believed, gathered, and stored. As you travel the path to your own gorgeousness notice the thoughts and feelings that arise.

You may experience thoughts and feelings that strengthen who you are and who you are becoming. Sometimes, you will have thoughts and feelings that do not support you. These thoughts and feelings are lies. Be willing to look at them. Be willing to release them if they no longer serve you.

Noticing our painful thoughts and emotions is essential. Without noticing, we will often suppress uncomfortable feelings and ideas without even realizing the impact they are having on us. Noticing means that we must be checked in to our body, not stuck or floating in our headspace.

The reason that we must be checked in to our physical body is because we cannot heal in our heads, in our minds. If we want a healing in our physical body we must have a physical body experience allowing ourselves to feel our body, our emotions and the thoughts which make us uncomfortable.

Being aware of and feeling these old ideas and emotions allows us to say goodbye to them with grace. Sometimes it is that easy; to notice them as they are leaving. For the more persistent thoughts and feelings, there is a simple process to release them.

This is the process for releasing uncomfortable thoughts and emotions: (Read this a couple of times and then do it from memory as best you can.)

Notice the uncomfortable thought or feeling, then identify it if you are able. For instance, a thought might be, "Who do you think you are?" Or, "You will never be able to do that!" You may be aware of where this idea originated but it is not important that you do so.

With a thought might come an adjacent feeling such as, sadness or anger, hopelessness or despair.

See if you can locate the source of this thought or feeling in your body.

If you can feel the location of the discomfort you may place your hands on your body in that location. If you can't locate the source of pain in your body then simply place your hands on your lower belly.

Acknowledge the thoughtform and discomfort that you are now willing to let go of.

See if it has something more to say to you. If appropriate, give it thanks for having protected you.

Breathe deeply with an emphasis on the exhale. Either breathe into the place where the pain originates or simply breathe into your belly. Imagine this energy of discomfort leaving your entire being as you exhale. Keep this up for a few minutes until you feel noticeably better or are at least in a state of peace.

Repeat this process if needed. As you release old worn out or toxic energies from your body, you are making room for new ideas, energy and light.

This releasing prepares you to embrace and then embody your beauty.

Finding your beauty.

"If you bring forth what is within you, what you bring forth will save you, If you do not bring forth what is within you, what you do not bring forth will destroy you."
—Jesus Christ, The Gospel of St. Thomas

Our unique beauty, our gift, is something that resonates deeply within. It ignites our passion and peacefulness, it is a quality that makes everything seem worthwhile. It makes us happy. Your particular beauty will be a quality, attribute or characteristic which is so much a part of your nature that you may need to dig a little bit to identify it. Characteristics that you see and admire in others may give you a clue about what most feels in sync with you. Often, when we admire something in another, it is because we have that very same or similar quality. Your personal beauty may have a tonal quality to it for you, like a song. Beauty itself may be your beauty.

Our mystical beauty becomes a power center within us from which we can operate in a more coherent fashion. When we are unsure of who we really are we create a life of chaos. When we know who we are, we are able to form around us coherent experiences and circumstances. In finding and owning our beauty we have a place from which we can build because we know what is essential to our own being. We become strong and grounded and more able to live from the inside outward instead of living just on the surface. Beauty, our own beauty, both softens and strengthens us, it creates lightness and depth. It protects our boundaries and opens us to love. Thus your beauty becomes your truth, your truth becomes your beauty.

To find your unique beauty, ponder these questions: What would you hope to be true about you?

How would you like for others to see you? What quality, talent or inherent essence do you wish was yours? What are the best things about you that have been told to you by others?

What would you secretly desire to be the truth about you? What quality of being or unique essence do you you sense about yourself?

What gifts do you wish to have? What would absolutely thrill you to hear about yourself? What strength, gift or gorgeousness do you possess?

Be open with yourself, explore a little bit. Here are some possibilities from an endless list. These may trigger you to find something that is missing from the list but belongs to you.

strength

power

love

wisdom

joy

healing

discipline

organizational skills

the ability to create beauty

peacemaking

deep heart listening

determination

constancy

loyalty

stamina

understanding

compassion

hard working

fun loving

tribal gatherer

artistic

creative

action taking

friendship

lover of all

kindness

presence

dignity

filled with abundance

hard core

luscious

laughter

perseverance

gentleness

fortitude

protectiveness

delight

perception

leadership

Any one of these attributes can generate powerful beauty in the interior castle of your being. We are honored for who we are, not just for what we do.

This is the process for finding your true beauty, your true essence:

Lotus breath: (Read this a couple of times and then do it from memory as best you can.)

Sit quietly. Check in with your body acknowledging the parts of you that are calling for attention.

Becoming comfortable, exhale while softening the mind and dropping into the body. Begin by breathing into your heart. Once you feel fully settled in the heart space, let the breath drop into the sacral bowl just below your navel. Move slowly and honor your body's process.

Place your attention and/or hands on your belly below your navel in the place of the sacral chakra. Feel or sense the sacral bowl forming a chalice into which you can receive. Continuing to breathe, send love into your body and your womb. Open yourself to receiving.

Acknowledge the loving being that is your true self, your Radiant Self, and her willingness to come forth to be seen and to help and guide you as you embrace, hear or sense her.

Listen to what she has to say to you.

Now ask; what is my beauty? What is my gift to the world and to myself? Trust yourself, feel into it, accept what you receive.

Breathe deeply and as you exhale, in your knowingness your beauty is _____.

Your particular beauty will have a protective power that strengthens you. Your true beauty, your inner beauty is your power. It is your super power.

What you see, sense, feel or receive is definitely what you get and what you get to receive. What you see is what you become. Your beauty becomes a light clarifying the pathways that are in front of you. Your beauty transmutes the old and outworn human consciousness into the gold of a more perfected, multi-faceted being. You become more of who you truly are. You become more of you.

Jesus, the Great Master, after healing the lame man at the pool at Bethesda said to him, "Take up thy bed and walk." In other words, it's done. Now let's get on with it, move forward and accept your healing. Jesus also said to the man that was healed, "Go and sin no more." 'Sinning' in this context is dipping back into the past, believing lies, revolving old thoughts and limitations.

When we find ourselves caught in the old mind traps and negative thought forms, it's time to re-center, to get in touch with our truth, remember who we are and engage our magic. The magic we perform is simply undoing the spells we cast upon ourselves.

We find our beauty.

Then, we clear all negativity or oppositional ideas and feelings to our embracing of this beauty.

We embody our beauty.

Now, seeing yourself for who you are, be willing to be seen by others as who you are. Do all things as her, the inner person that is in full command of her power, beauty, and radiance. We now bathe in our own delicious worthiness and lusciousness, transmitting our inner blessings into the world around us. As we move through our environment, broadcasting our beauty, others are given permission to shine in the same way. Inner and outer beauty coming together, the equation is squared, magnified and becomes the rarefied essence of our Magic Presence. We change, we change the world. Now our service begins.

Walk in power, walk in your beauty.

"Let the beauty we love be what we do, there are a thousand ways to kneel and kiss the ground."
—Rumi

About the Author

Carol DeFrancisco is the founder of FireHeart Nation, a company that is transforming the lives and businesses of entrepreneurs and executives by providing a roadmap for people to align with their true purpose, achieve their highest vision and create extraordinary happiness.

Carol's unique "FireHeart Creation Process" has assisted people around the world in exceeding their personal and financial goals using FireHeart Technology to access their heart's intelligence.

She is passionate about women's empowerment, conducting workshops and seminars in North America and around the world and is inspired to be involved with women who are revolutionizing themselves.

Carol also applies her expertise to the field of racial justice and the healing of racialized trauma, another of her passions.

Carol graduated from Western Illinois University with a Bachelor of Fine Arts. She is driven daily by helping people to find their true beauty and personal power.

Carol is available for personal consultation, workshops and speaking engagements.

www.fireheartnation.com
carol@fireheartnation.com
@openaslove
Carol DeFrancisco Facebook/ Messenger

FIVE

Dr. Marion Gibbon

AS IN NATURE, THE END MAKES WAY FOR A NEW
BEGINNING

We live in a world where most of the top echelons are male, but I believe we are on the cusp of a societal paradigm shift. The leadership models must move from dominion, autocracy, and male-dominated knowledge to a more feminine approach. It is time we move away from "wielding power over others" and the requirement that leadership be charismatic- and ego-driven. The shift may be somewhat uncomfortable because of the clash between familiar old ways and the shift to the feminine model.

A more feminine approach to leadership is becoming apparent. A few tender shoots of ideas are incredibly small and fragile but extremely important. Female leaders like New Zealand's Jacinda Ardern, Former Chancellor of Germany Angela Merkel, and others have been effective through the pandemic and have shown the strengths of the new feminine leadership. Deaths due to COVID-19 were fewer in their countries, and these leaders brought their people with them rather than telling them what to do. As of May 2020, New Zealand had roughly 1,500 cases of COVID-19 and fewer than two dozen deaths, according to NPR.[1]

In September 2009 at the Vancouver Peace Summit, the Dalai Lama said, "The world will be saved by the Western women." I feel that there is a caveat to that statement as I see this more as the women who have awakened into their feminine power.

Like so many other white, straight, cis-gender, able-bodied, neuro-diverse, mentally healthyish, middle-class women around me, I am incredibly privileged, more so than many women who walk this earth. So, why do we still feel powerless to make change?

I feel it is because we do too much, we rush, feel unworthy, ashamed, and our to-do lists are so long. We don't put ourselves forward because of our "perceived lacks." If we believe in ourselves and that we are "good enough." we can achieve what is our central most desire. There is a need to slow down in order to be more open and awake. Our collective feminine awakening will lead us into a better world where there is more caring, more connectivity, and where communities support each other.

Feminine Archetypes

I first came across the feminine archetypes in 2019. I had started doing research for a book on feminine leadership and saw Cyndie's book. I later had a conversation with her and realised how this thinking could be useful in coaching and enabling others to become their best possible self. I went on to take her archetype quiz and at that time the butterfly was my mentor, extremely creative, and just beginning to express myself more fully. It was interesting as I also have a movement practice and my friends saw me as a "butterfly in a bell jar." I have recently taken the quiz again and now find that my primary archetype is that of the hummingbird. As a hummingbird you embody love, joy, and unity as your core feminine essence.

What was I seeking?

I have been on a journey that arose out of a desire to be happier in my own body and to be confident in speaking out when I saw injustice.

My multiple professional spheres have enabled me to become more aware and grow into the person I am today. I have found a place where I can contribute to the world becoming a better place.

Who have been some of the most important influences in my life?

I have had the opportunity to meet some incredible women over the course of my career. I started out in education as a teacher due to my biology teacher, Miss Rock. She was an inspiration who awoke in me my love of nature and concern for the planet. Whilst on that path I went to Africa and learned of the nutritional deficiencies that many children face. I met an inspirational teacher called Ardy Keilmann and that led me to undertake a further qualification at the London School of Medicine and Tropical Medicine. I had some amazing teachers who have been a strong influence in my life and who led me to go to work internationally on completion of my master's in public health nutrition.

In Sri Lanka, I worked with Prof. Piriyani Soysa and learned so much from the women I interacted with. After Sri Lanka, I went back to Kenya and then to Nepal. In Nepal I worked with some incredible people, all of whom have influenced my work. Durga Pokhrel who worked to establish equal rights for women and other excluded groups in Nepal. She was a star that shined brightly but sadly passed away last year. The women I interviewed for my book have all had an important part to play in my life. Some of them I have known for a long time, and others are newer friends.

Appreciation

If there is one thing I wish more people knew or appreciated about me it would be how being neurodivergent can actually be a "super power". It enables you to see things in a different way and brings a heightened sense of creativity to every situation.

Coming Home to Myself

In hummingbird consciousness, we engage from the level of the soul, just as that tiny bird finds the valour to take this monumental journey, we can discover the courage to perceive our own lives as a journey of growth and discovery, of spiritual maturation, we don't fuss about the details of our flight because we feel confident that regardless of what the weather is over north Carolina or how few resting spots there will be as we travel across the gulf of Mexico, we will make it to our destination.

–From *Courageous Dreaming* by Alberto Villoldo

Taking on the archetypes within body, heart, and soul (embodiment) makes you become your true self. Knowing yourself from the inside out means that you can bring your dreams into being. It allows your creativity and intuition to be tools for you to have a deeper sense of knowing where you are heading, and as a result, your desires are realised.

I have found understanding my archetype of the hummingbird has highlighted aspects of myself and enabled me to help others to blossom and become more visible.

Finding My Purpose in Life

The current crisis across the globe is underlining that there is a need for radical change. Changes in biodiversity and climate change are two such areas to consider. To illustrate the degree of biodiversity loss, it is estimated that the species loss we are facing now is between one thousand and ten thousand times higher than the *natural extinction rate*.[2]

- The World Wildlife Fund calculates that between 0.01 and 0.1 percent of all species become extinct each year.

- There are different estimates of how many species there are on Earth, but the minimum loss rate means between two hundred and two thousand extinctions occur every year.
- If the upper estimate of species numbers is true—that there are one hundred million different species coexisting with us on our planet—then between ten thousand and one hundred thousand species are becoming extinct each year.

To reduce exploitation, there is a need to redefine how we consider our economy. The linear economy we currently use is made up of the following steps: extract, produce, consume, and throw away; hence being known as the "throw away society". The linear approach to the economy tends to involve autocratic leadership where the power is held at the top of the pyramid. The new form of leadership will be more caring, compassionate, and creative, more on that later.

What is taking place is a reconsideration of the economy into something that is kinder and will not lead to the death of humanity. This form of thinking is called the circular economy.

Defining what is meant by "circular economy" is important, and there are varying definitions, but the concept that underpins it is that it is restorative and eliminates waste through better materials, products, and systems design, enabled by innovative business models.

The circular economy is based on three principles, driven by design:

- Eliminate waste and pollution — **Reduce**
- Circulate products and materials rather than continually make new ones — **Re-use** and
- Regenerate nature — **Recycle** and **re-plant**

The approach requires a transition to renewable energy and material and decouples economic activity from the consumption of the finite resources we have on and within our planet. It is a resilient system that is good for business, people, and the environment. The biggest change with this economic way of thinking is that "growth" of the economy is not the be all and end all, rather, it is how can we live within our means without exploiting our planet's resources. Basically, it is a production and consumption model that ensures sustainability in that we can optimise resources, reduce the exploitation and over-consumption of raw materials, and recover waste by recycling or giving it a second life as a new product. The idea arises from imitating nature's feedback loops, where everything has value and everything is used, where waste becomes a new resource. In this way, the balance between progress and sustainability is maintained.

Many people are aware of the foregoing three principles, but there are a further four to consider, making a total of seven Rs:

1. **Redesign:** Creating and designing products using a manufacturing process that uses fewer raw materials, extends their lifecycle, and generates less waste (or at least waste that is easier to recycle). This improves protection of our environment.
2. **Reduce:** Change our consumption habits towards a more sustainable model. If we reduce consumption, we avoid the generation of waste, the use of raw materials, and therefore reduce the impact on the environment.
3. **Reuse:** Reuse or repurpose products to extend their lifecycle.
4. **Repair:** Until recently, when something broke, we tended to replace it. However, repairing it is not only cheaper but also avoids the use of new raw materials, saves energy, and does not generate environmental waste.
5. **Renovate:** Update old objects so that they can be reused as vintage, e.g. furniture, clothing.
6. **Recycle:** Promote best practice in waste management and use what you can as raw material to manufacture new products.
7. **Recover:** Give new uses to products that are going to be discarded, for example, using plastic bottles to make other products like insulation materials. Some companies are beginning to recompense customers who want to upgrade and reuse some of the components.

Being kinder to the planet is the starting point for the new model of leadership. The components and qualities of leadership need to change from the old paradigm of leadership to one of a more embodied, empathetic one.

Old	New
Autocratic	Caring and compassionate
Rule based with boundaries	Creativity and innovation
Hierarchical	Networked
Power over	Power within
Who you know	What you know
Command and control	Open and empowering
Secrecy and competition	Cooperation and connection

Table 1. Out with the Old and In with the New

It is critical that attributes of the new leadership are embodied and consist of thirteen qualities, some of these are indicated in the following list:

- Caring
- Compassionate
- Courageous
- Characterful
- Communicator
- Connected
- Community focused

What I mean by "embodied" is where you are able to tangibly bring your whole self into your way of being, which means bringing in your mind, body, and spirit into who you are. It involves feeling at home in your body, being connected to both your interior and exterior world, in the present moment, and being able to feel all your sensations and feelings and that you are able to safely express your needs, desires, and wants in an appropriate fashion.

We are living in a time when it appears that caring is not central to our way of life. The media portrays a world that is careering towards self-destruction and yet there are some that are concerned about minimising their footprint, living in tune with earth's cycles, and not exploiting the planet's resources. Our workplaces are often highly toxic and lead to burnout and stress as a result of high workloads. Through the pandemic there were tentative changes to improve staff wellbeing, but these are now receding with the requirement for a return to the office, and the trust gained is now receding. The courage to continue to advocate for staff wellbeing and improved conditions needs to continue unabated.

If you want those who work for you to accomplish great things, you must show them who you truly are. Caring leadership contains a set of five core values:[3]

1. Always lead with kindness, compassion, and equality, and I go further to include equity.
2. Generate hope and faith through co-creation.
3. Actively innovate with insight, reflection, and wisdom.
4. Purposely create protected space that is founded on mutual respect and a caring nature.
5. Embody an environment of caring – trusting for self and others.

You notice the inter-linkages of caring and compassion and the importance of protected spaces that allow conversations that are heartfelt and authentic. This takes courage to fly in the face of the current values and expectations that are seen as important in a world based on a different set of values. It requires us to have character where integrity, truthfulness, and authenticity are central rather than ego and lies.

Being connected is the way we get on in life. There are very few things that we can do entirely on our own. As the saying goes, no man is an island. Those from deprived backgrounds have far less connections, and this leads to challenges in getting work and progressing in their careers. If we are to reduce inequities, there is a real need to consider how we alleviate some of the barriers that people from the global majority and more impoverished communities face. It is for this reason that we need to involve communities in the co-creation and co-production of opportunities to overcome such barriers.

Establishing Circles of Empowerment and Connection

In a world where women still face bias and other barriers at work, circles are a safe space to share your struggles, give and get advice, and celebrate each other's wins. Whether you need help navigating your new normal at work or are looking for support from women who understand what you're going through, joining a circle will give everyone the boost we all need.

Circles bring together women from all walks of life, from asylum seekers, refugees, and women whose children have just started school to women whose children have "left the nest" and female entrepreneurs. In these small groups, women get and give peer mentorship, sharpen their skills, and have a place to be unapologetically ambitious.

I find the support gained from having like-minded women to discuss ideas and plan together immeasurable. How might joining a community or having safe spaces for conversation and dialogue help you in your life?

Call to Action

What is it that you will take forward? There are several options:

1. Make changes to how you live your life:

   a. Reduce
   b. Recycle
   c. Reuse

2. Review your leadership and consider what aspects that you want to focus on and develop.

3. Establish or join a "Circle of Empowerment and Connection".

I am committed to having a discussion with my husband to consider how we can have less of an impact on our planet, so that we can tread more softly.

---

1. https://www.npr.org/sections/goatsandsoda/2020/05/23/861577367/messaging-from-leaders-who-have-tamed-their-countrys-coronavirus-outbreaks
2. The natural extinction rate is what would be expected without man on Earth and is known as the background extinction rate.
3. Williams, R, McDowell, J, Kautz, D (2011) A Caring Leadership Model for Nursing's Future. *International Journal for Human Caring* 15(1): 31–35.

About the Author

Marion's career has been a portfolio. She worked in many fields and can speak their languages. Marion's chapter focuses on the need for a new form of leadership in these changing times. She initially trained as a teacher and taught biology, science, and art. After completing a year of teaching in Surrey, she took up a teaching post in Kenya. Living in Thika, she taught for three years and gained an interest in nutrition.

Studying nutrition at London's School of Hygiene and Tropical Medicine led to a post with the school as a researcher in Sri Lanka working with preschool education and nutrition. The following year she moved to Kenya, where she worked with malnourished children and their families. While there, she had her first child; the family then moved to Nepal. There she had her second daughter and undertook a doctorate that focused on women's health and empowerment.

Back in England after over ten years overseas, she worked in academia and the National Health Service. Through the NHS she became a consultant in public health and trained as a coach. Marion continues to work in public health in a local authority in the Midlands, UK. She is also an artist who uses creativity in coaching. Marion published a book on embodied leadership during which she interviewed some of the incredible women she met over the course of her career.

https://www.mariongibbon.com

instagram.com/marion_gibbon
linkedin.com/in/marion-gibbon-b5805617
amazon.com/dp/B08R4FB331

SIX

Anna Koskinaris

BE TRUE TO YOURSELF, LIVE IN AUTHENTICITY, AND BECOME YOUR OWN HEROINE

*G*rowing up, I was often the shy, observant type. I watched classmates and friends in school act silly and get into trouble, and I saw how their behavior was characterized by external influences. Influence from peers, adults, caretakers, and society in general. I fought hard not to be affected or influenced by peer pressure, but there are a few times I recall when I didn't succeed. I would often feel otherworldly, that I didn't fit the mold of my peers. At first, I felt it was because of my very traditional Greek upbringing. My parents migrated from Greece and worked very hard, day and night to provide for the needs of our family. When my loving and respected parents were absent for work, my maternal grandmother who left Greece as a widow came to the US to care for and watch over my brother and me. During her care, she taught me to be kind to others and not ever judge anyone because we haven't walked in others' shoes or know the struggles others face. I didn't want to do what all my peers were doing. I didn't want to follow trends. I didn't want to do things just because others did. I was just not interested in behaving or doing the same as others. There were times I was viewed as a rebel by members of my family, at school, and early on in my career. When I thought about why I didn't want to be like others, I realized I wouldn't be who I really was, only how others wanted me to be. I wanted to be genuine and just be myself. At school and in my neighborhood, I made friends easily. Heck, I had friends from all walks of life. Many people approached me and told me things they felt, some very personal, that I hadn't ever known to ask them. I always listened to them, sometimes with sincere compassion showing through my facial expressions and other times I had no response, and that was okay.

When I was in seventh grade, bullies began bullying one group of my friends. Eventually, they started to try and bully me. I stood firm, expressing myself through words and compassion, and defended myself. I did not threaten or carry out physical harm, which was something my friends and I with. I realized then, after much observation and eventually becoming friends with many of them, those bullies came from troubled, volatile, and abusive homes. I began to feel a heavy sadness radiate through me when I learned this. The same bullies never tried to bully my friends or me again after that last confrontation. It wasn't often that we'd run into them and other bullies during school.

Interestingly, weeks later, a couple of different bullies were in the hallway next to their lockers. My friends and I started walking down the hallway toward them to get to our history class. One of the bullies burst out crying as we approached them. We asked if they were okay. We didn't hear a response and paused for a moment. Then I said, "I know something is bothering you."

The bell rang and class was starting. I didn't move and knew I was going to be late for class. My friends hurried on to get to class and said we'll meet up afterward. The bully, her name was Tonya, started talking about the hurt she was feeling inside from her abuse as a child. I listened and stayed with her for a little while. I said, "I'm your friend."

Later that year, we all became good friends. This was the defining moment in my life when I felt I needed to be true to myself and become my own heroine. Essentially, this was done by cultivating and understanding my self-awareness and inner strength to help others achieve the same.

Fast forward, past high school and into my early twenties, I met my best friend Bettina at my workplace. I would never have guessed then how my life would be significantly impacted by our meeting. We both worked in customer service for a newspaper publication. I started with the company a few months before Bettina. The company was growing rapidly, and they hired a few more full-time representatives to answer customer calls. Bettina was hired and assigned to work in the cubicle right behind me. In the beginning, I remembered she was loud, but not on purpose. Her voice carried over when she spoke. Bettina was lively, with a cheerful and captivating personality and a very strong presence. We would be able to hear each other on phone calls with customers and comment afterward about our calls and how we handled the problems of customers who called into our department. Bettina and I would often receive awards as the top-rated customer service associates out of twenty for our department. We both competed for the top ranking but always in a healthy and friendly manner. Our service ratings were based on overall customer satisfaction, which included follow through and retention or repeat business. It was fascinating to me that we always matched our ratings results for providing the most friendly, honest, patient, empathetic, and helpful service to customers. We surprised management with how often we achieved the same results.

Of the two of us, I was always the quieter, soft-spoken one. When Bettina and I became great friends, that all changed. Bettina was going through a divorce at the time we met, and I could sense it affected her without her talking about it. Behind her infectious smile, super contagious laugh, and one-of-a-kind witty humor, I sensed Bettina was extremely distressed. At the time I felt helpless. I felt I could do more than lend an ear and offer a hug when Bettina decided to share with me what was going on in her life. I remember saying to her, "I have no idea what you're going through," and "I feel I could say or do more to help but don't know what." That's when I heard for the first time the words, "Be true to yourself, mori." We had our code words, often informal Greek adjectives we used in place of calling out each other's name in public. *Mori* was our code word for friend. Bettina was saying to be my authentic self, to not be or respond as someone I am not or how I thought she needed me to be, and to show her in my own way that I am her friend. Bettina's words never left me. I never looked back.

Of the many and apparent reasons Bettina and I shared a symbiotic, understanding, sustainable, and cohesive friendship over the years is the fact that she and I were practically "late bloomers" in life. We both started and graduated from college later in our adult years and started our chosen careers then. I didn't follow tradition or heed my parents' advice to go to college immediately after high school. I didn't have clarity then of what profession I wanted to get into, and I didn't want to go to college just to go because it was the norm. Bettina and I both became involved in long-term romantic relationships around the same time. We experienced injustices, setbacks, heartaches, and headaches, discussed them together and often dealt with what we experienced in the same manner. Through all these experiences, Bettina and I knew the meaning of being true to ourselves and the significance it had for ourselves and in our relationships and why it mattered to show up in this way.

Years and life experiences later, I recall Bettina's words in my mind when I need a good and swift reminder for how to respond to setbacks, misunderstandings, and conflict. I remember feeling that I had to "prove" myself to others who didn't or hardly knew me or what my life was like for me at the time. I responded and chose to express myself authentically, to show my true self with dignity, compassion, and soul and to stand up for what I believe and know to be my truth. I turned away from friends, colleagues, and relatives when they didn't agree, appreciate, or see me as my true self. When this happened, I felt a profound liberation and essence for cultivating deep inner strength, continual self-awareness, and self-acceptance. Acceptance that always led me to awareness. Awareness that led me to understanding. Understanding that led me to resilience. Resilience that led me to find inner strength and heal. Healing that led me to liberation and resolve. Liberation that led me to being my own heroine and best friend.

I'll never forget that day in August 2013 when I received a phone call from Bettina; she was hardly able to speak when I answered her call cheerfully. I heard her murmur the words after what seemed like a long pause followed by a distraught sigh, "I have cancer." I felt my inner world in a flash of a moment literally crumble. I had the wind knocked out of me. Bettina said she had to go and couldn't talk further. I expressed to Bettina how sorry I was to receive the news but mustered the strength to say we will get through this, then we ended the call. I couldn't breathe. I couldn't look where I was going, my eyes welled up about to burst at the seams. I needed to hold myself together until I found the nearest hideaway spot. I was walking down a sidewalk on a busy afternoon in downtown Berkeley near the college campus when I answered Bettina's call. I was wearing sunglasses. I recall it was an exceptionally warm day out, but my body suddenly felt even warmer. I felt what I heard described as an electric shock. I was only a block away from my car, which was parked inside a public garage. I kept walking toward the garage with my head slightly down, looking up only so I wouldn't miss the entrance to the garage, but I struggled to hold myself together. It felt like an eternity, the longest walk to my parked car. I hurried to get into my car, shut the door, then decided to move my car to another vacant parking space, nowhere near other parked cars or the stairs. I drove a couple levels up to find a shaded vacant space, parked my car, reclined my seat slightly, cracked a couple of windows open, and just let it out. I kept my sunglasses on, wiping the tears rolling down my face and stayed in my car until I felt ready to breathe and move again. I left the garage an hour later.

The news from Bettina hit me hard. I was devastated and felt helpless. At the time of this news, Bettina was living in Michigan, and I was living in Northern California. I heard less and less from Bettina right after that phone call. I knew she was dealing with a lot. It was difficult not to hear from her or know what was going on with her during that time. I called to check on her occasionally and left voicemail messages that mostly went unanswered. I knew she was trying to handle the news and prognosis as best as she could and begin treatment.

December of that year, I hadn't heard from Bettina since we last talked on the phone. She called me about the middle of the month to wish me a Merry Christmas. She knew she'd be undergoing treatment, which included radiation and chemotherapy, and she didn't know when we'd be speaking again. About forty days after that call, I heard from Bettina again. This time, she sounded so cheerful on the phone. I was extremely happy to hear from her. I couldn't wait to hear her tell me her prognosis following the recent treatments she received the month before.

Before I could speak, Bettina said, "They got the cancer, I am cancer-free and now going into remission!" I immediately felt a heavy weight lift off my shoulders and breathed a huge sigh of relief when she told me the miraculous news.

Bettina and I remained in contact with each other more regularly after that. We would often text brief greetings and notes. It seemed that even though we were not physically located near one another, we were still very spiritually near and attuned to what was going on in our lives. What seemed like merely days, a few more months had gone by. One late afternoon in May, I called Bettina at our usual time. Bettina sounded unusually deflated on the phone. We shared some small talk and updates about our lives, then she told me the cancer was back. My mind started racing. I started to question, what, why, how, when? I couldn't organize my thoughts fast enough as I was listening to Bettina speak. We agreed to end the call when Bettina said she didn't want to talk more about it then. She was in the middle of getting dinner ready for herself and others. I thought I was literally having a nightmare, only I was awake, and it was real. I didn't speak with Bettina again for several days. I thought at that point, I really didn't know what was going to happen and started to think about visiting her in Michigan. The days approached with a strange sense of unknowing and an uneasy feeling that I had to leave very soon to see Bettina. I thought to myself, *If not now, I don't know when I might see her again.* I booked my flight from SFO to Michigan to leave in two days. I would take a few days off from work. It was all I had available to take, and whether or not it was unpaid, it didn't matter. As a matter of fact, nothing else mattered to me more at that time than going to see my best friend. My partner at the time would watch over the pets. I did what I needed and was right for me to do. I was being true to myself and a true friend.

It was June. I booked an early morning non-stop flight to Detroit. It was a full flight. I remember sitting next to a family of four with two young children.

One of the boys turned toward me and asked, "Where are you going?"

I guessed he was six years old. I answered, "I am going to see my friend."

The young boy looked at me and smiled and said, "Yay!"

Then his mother said, "Sorry, miss, he's really talkative."

I looked at her with a smile and said, "It's okay, I enjoy him talking."

She giggled slightly and said, "Thank you."

The entire flight the young boy glanced toward me and smiled. I smiled back. I have always been one who "connects the dots," finding "signs" and meaning from my experiences and random exchanges with strangers and others. Bettina was the more talkative one between us, and she always wore a contagious and beautiful smile.

When we arrived in Detroit, just as we were deboarding the plane, the young boy said, "I hope you have fun with your friend, bye!"

I winked and responded to him, "Thank you, I will. Keep smiling. Bye for now." I held the tears back from my eyes. That young boy's message, whether he knew it or not, made a profound and lasting impact in my life. He knew what mattered the most.

Bettina and her fiancé knew of my arrival and had offered for me to stay in their spare bedroom. I learned then that Bettina was bedridden most of the time and not in a coherent frame of mind to even recognize the time of day and her surroundings. She was experiencing a lot of pain often and the chemo knocked her out. I rented a car at the airport and drove to their home an hour away. I was getting very hungry. I hadn't eaten since dinner the night before, almost eighteen hours ago. I managed to stay hydrated by drinking a lot of water. I quickly remembered having visited the area several times in the past. There was Greektown in downtown Detroit. I did a Yelp search online for a nearby popular Greek restaurant in Detroit since I'd be driving through the city to get to Bettina and her fiancé's home. I located Pegasus Taverna. I called the restaurant to ask if I could place an order for pickup. I was twenty minutes away and wanted to provide them enough time to prepare the order. I really did not want to delay a single minute more getting to see my best friend. I knew every minute counted. I placed an order for our favorite Greek appetizer, flamed saganaki cheese, a couple bowls of avgolemono soup, homemade village bread loaf, and a Greek chicken entrée for Bettina. When I arrived at the restaurant to stop in and pay for the order and leave, the host who rang up my order asked me if it would be long before I got to enjoy the food. She wanted to make sure the bread didn't get soggy and secured the containers a little more so the food wouldn't get cold. After I shared with her where I was headed, I mentioned that I was from out of town visiting my friend.

The host responded and said, "Oh, that's so nice. You are bringing dinner over." I felt compelled to explain further why I was in the area and that it was the least I could do.

She and I both started to get teary eyed when I told her my purpose for being in town. She gave me a hug and said, "You're a real good friend."

I said, "Thank you. Thank you for your support, and so are you." I left the restaurant. I had another thirty-five minutes or more of driving time until my arrival at Bettina's home. My adrenaline was rising. All I could think about was having time with Bettina after so many years.

It was early evening on a beautiful late spring day when I pulled into the driveway of Bettina's home. I got out of the car, grabbed my purse, our dinner, and left my suitcase and other belongings in the car and locked it. The side door to the house next to the driveway was left unlocked for me. As I walked silently through the kitchen and through the hallway to the bedrooms, I looked to the right and saw Bettina in bed, slightly awake. The room was dark. She was the only one home for a brief while when I arrived. I went up to Bettina and said, "Hi, Mori," and hugged her where she lay. Bettina expressed her happiness to see me and tried to hug me back.

I sat down on the chair next to her bed where she lay. Bettina was dozing on and off and smiled when she woke up and saw me. I let her know I brought her favorite Greek food for dinner. She smiled and said, "Oh, thank you so much." My main thoughts were for her to feel comfortable and eat her dinner. She sat up in her bed to start eating. She didn't eat much. I put away the tray with her dinner and let her know it was placed on the nightstand next to her bed in case she got hungry and wanted to eat again. There was a glass of water and juice with a straw on the nightstand. I would ask her occasionally if she wanted a drink and then hand her the glass with the straw if she said yes. Whether we talked or not was up to her. I simply wanted to be there with her. Her fiancé came home shortly after I arrived. It was my first time meeting him. He was a nice and welcoming gentleman who cared deeply for Bettina. He showed me where the bathroom and my bedroom were. After a little time passed, I went out to the rental car and grabbed the rest of my belongings and brought them inside into my bedroom. I unpacked some and got ready for bed. I said goodnight to Bettina and her fiancé.

The next day, I woke up as Bettina's fiancé was getting ready to leave for work. He said, "Please make yourself feel at home and feel free to cook and use the kitchen." I asked him about Bettina's dietary needs. He said, "She can eat what was in the fridge and pantry, and there are a few things you might need to cook and bring to her to eat in bed, some juice and water."

I decided to stock up on fresh fruit and vegetables. I looked up the nearest store to make a quick grocery run. Bettina wouldn't eat much, and some of her food was liquefied in the blender to make it easier for her to digest. I came back to their house and put away the grocery items. I went to check on Bettina and ask her if she wanted something to eat and brought her some water. Bettina hadn't moved much from where she was lying on the bed. Her bedroom was dark during the daytime. She had all the blinds closed and did not want any light or sun to shine through. I asked her if she was comfortable, and she murmured yes but said she was in pain. I asked her if she wanted to eat. She said yes and then asked for an Italian beef sandwich from Portillo's. That was one of her favorite food items she'd order when we'd go out to eat at Portillo's in the past. I looked up the nearest Portillo's and placed an order for pick up. Once I returned home with the order, I could tell Bettina was working up an appetite and began eating her sandwich. I was really happy to see Bettina eat. She had lost a lot of weight during her treatments.

The next couple of days went by. I stayed with Bettina the entire time throughout my visit with her. We talked a little, ate together, and watched movies. At one point, Bettina asked me to look online for what diet she should be following. We looked up the information together on her laptop computer and the recommended diet was rich in fruits and vegetables. Bettina asked if there were any of these food items in the kitchen. I said yes and brought her some fruit that she asked for. A couple more days went by, and I had to return back home to the Bay Area. I left my visit with Bettina and her fiancé with a heavy heart. A heavy heart because I missed her after all these years and because this time I didn't know if I would see her again. Bettina's fiancé and close friend who lived nearby were caring for and watching her. They said her oncologists were uncertain whether the chemo would be effective in treating ridding her of the cancer. I kissed and hugged Bettina so tightly before I left.

My flight back home felt like the longest non-stop flight ever. I fought back the tears in my eyes during the flight and wore my sunglasses the entire time onboard. I arrived back home and every day after my return, I would call and talk with Bettina, even if it was only for a few minutes. In the past, Bettina and I would be on the phone talking for hours. She always brought a sense of humor into all our conversations; she was truly gifted in making others laugh, even the most stoic personalities. After Bettina began chemo treatments, it was difficult for her to carry out conversations and be her usual cheery self. I knew then that I needed to bring the cheer to her. I needed to be strong for her and be her pillar of strength and courage. I needed to let her know that no matter what, I was going to be there for her, and I was going to show up as my authentic, true self, best friend, and heroine. And I did, I was, and to this day I am my own best friend and heroine living my life with authenticity and being my true self.

Two months after my visit, Bettina was placed into hospice care. Within several short days she passed on. I will never forget the call I received, what I was doing, where I was, and how I felt when I received that call. I was in denial. I couldn't accept what I was hearing and what I was being told. There was no way in hell I could. I collapsed on the sidewalk outside where I was walking my dog. I tried so hard to get myself back up. My dog didn't know what came over me. Minutes later, a lovely and friendly couple walked by, and the man said to me, "How did you survive the earthquake?"

He was referring to the earthquake that happened in Napa a couple of days prior. I responded and said, "I am doing okay, thanks, and how did you both do?" He didn't notice the shakiness in my voice from the news I had just received.

What he said next, I believe was spiritually intended for me to hear. He said, "There's a silver lining in it. We survived, and it fills us with gratitude and appreciation." The couple smiled and began walking again.

I said, "Thank you, really, thank you for that and enjoy your walk." I believed it wasn't a mere coincidence running into that couple and having that brief, yet miraculous encounter. Luckily, my dog and I were only a couple of blocks away from home. We walked back a little quicker than usual. Soon after I got home, I took off my dog's leash, went upstairs, kneeled down on the bedroom floor, and let it all out.

Bettina and I had plans. We planned to visit Greece together. She had never been. She wanted to meet my extended Greek family and enjoy our favorite Greek dishes together. Bettina often talked about us getting old and still hanging out on the porch and cracking jokes about some of our wild encounters, memorable experiences, and our friendship. Since Bettina's passing, it's taken some time to grieve and heal while also celebrating her life as she would have wanted me to do.

What I learned about being true to myself is that it's up to you, and only you how you express and show up for yourself. Your character will be judged, your resolve will be tested, others will not understand you or accept you, you may question the status quo, you will not feel the need to compare yourself to others, there's no room or time for envy, competition, pettiness, gossip, or greed. You're curious, you're unique, you live your life with understanding and peace from within. You are kind to yourself and others. You are happy knowing that you have nothing to prove to anyone, liberated because you're not living a lie. You respect your self-worth, set boundaries in order to not be taken for granted, speak your truth, practice self-care, maintain a healthy and positive attitude, develop inner strength and knowledge, and become your own heroine.

In honor of Bettina, my best friend, and the wonderful authors and collaborators of this book, I welcome you to refer back to this book and chapter anytime. In a world of fake news, fake people, fake many things, it is important more now than ever to live with authenticity. When you are feeling that there is not anyone in your life who is standing by you, who supports you living your life with authenticity, you can always know that whether we meet or not, however far or near, somewhere in this vast yet small world, I will be cheering you on while you are being your true you.

About the Author

Anna Koskinaris is an author, coach, healer, cross-cultural communicator, mentor, emotional intelligence practitioner and promoter, holistic wellness advocate, entrepreneur, professional dancer, and investor. Anna operated and co-owned a private Montessori school, worked in education sales and management, technology, was a behavior therapist for autistic children, and worked for years in customer-facing roles. She enjoys creative expression and the arts, and she is passionate about the outdoors, science, animals, kids, exercise, jumprope, and playing tennis. She also has a rare knack for identifying and bringing out the best in others.

Anna is an unwavering proponent and student of lifelong learning and personal development. She has a unique and uncanny ability to put others at ease through her calming presence and accepting personality. Anna's listening skills are second to none.

She is exceptionally intuitive, kind, intelligent, resourceful, patient, empathic, friendly, and fair-minded. She has traveled to twenty-three countries and speaks three languages. Anna has a BA in marketing and business from DePaul University and an associates in early childhood education from the University of Phoenix, and she is certified in Montessori. She was born and raised in the Midwest, spent many summers in Europe, and divides her time living in the San Francisco Bay Area and visiting family and friends in the Midwest and Greece.

Email: koskinaris.anna@gmail.com

linkedin.com/in/anna-k-17b7b425

SEVEN

Judy McNutt

EMBODY YOUR INTUITION, CHANGE YOUR LIFE

J ask you to begin by imagining your ancestors' day-to-day lives. How few of them ever thought about themselves or how they felt? Did any of them acknowledge inner knowing or intuition? Was it safe for them to admit, let alone act on their intuition? For most of them, life was about survival, family, community, and safe relationships. We may believe society is more open-minded now, but what has truly changed? I'll grant you that our great-grandmothers might wonder what we do now that modern conveniences have left us with all this "extra time" on our hands. But have modern amenities only freed us up for longer to-do lists, more responsibility, and **greater separation from our "inner truth?"**

Significant Questions About the Lives of Women Remain:

- How safe are we in our relationships?
- What is our pathway to sovereignty and security?
- How do we feel when we speak of using our intuition?
- Do we embody truth to live life fully expressed?

Would Grandmother's answers to these questions be different from yours?

- From whom do you hide your true nature?
- What are you not saying and have not thought about in years?
- What are you choosing not to see or hear?
- What can you no longer stomach?
- Do you feel like a possession or a free and sovereign being?
- What is the current state of a once-most-trusted relationship?
- Are you unconditionally loved and satisfied with life?
- Do you feel empowered? Safe?
- Is your intuition a trusted tool or someone else's eye-rolling idea of coincidence or "luck"?
- Have you repeatedly ignored "gut feelings"?

The Intuition Gap

Just like our ancestors, the intuition gap in our lives often begins at a young age. When the people closest to us betray our trust or fail to recognize our intuitive abilities and unique gifts, it can create vulnerabilities and trigger painful memories that hinder our well-being. Society's emphasis on practical matters and material success can also lead us further away from what truly matters.

The Stories

I am profoundly grateful and humbled to share the stories of my soulmate clients and the courageous women who have allowed me to be a part of their journey. Each story comes from my experience coaching clients intuitively writing their books or women who have bravely shared their journeys with me.

From the forthcoming author of The Six Steps to Recovery from Domestic Violence, Aurora Suzanne—"*In my efforts to please my mother, I ran the sewing machine needle through my finger. Frustrated with me because I had no talent for either cooking or sewing, she said, 'You'll never please a man!' I had a flicker of intuition that her statement was false, but it stuck with me, and I began to believe that sex was the only way I could have a relationship with a man, which paved the way for sexual abuse."*

Our mothers gave us life, and, for better or worse, they passed along the mothering they inherited from their mothers.

My friend Joy S. shares a stark revelation: *"I grew up with a mother who made it clear she didn't much like me. Unsurprisingly, I ended up with a similar husband. He even tried to kill me."*

Some experiences serve to awaken our gifts and superpowers. But, like a fear-filled birth, awakening to the truth can be noisy, messy, toxic, dangerous, and even life-threatening.

Please know I have not set out to blame anybody for anything, but can you feel a part of yourself in their stories? Read on.

So What Is It You Didn't Get?

Did controlling adults shun, belittle, or shut down your intuition? Were your feelings or assessments deemed wrong or crazy? How could you have understood the truth about relationships?

Our intuition continuously warns of danger, and we hear stories of those who wish they had listened to that inner voice. But instead, ignorance, suppression, and damaged egos have forced us to live in a web of delusion and deception instead of forming healthy relationships.

Forthcoming author of "You Think You Know Me," Yvonne A's story.

"'BUT MAMA,' I pleaded, 'This is a mistake. I don't want to marry him.'

'Too bad. You should have thought of that before you got pregnant,' she shouted, jerking me around to the mirror to fix my stupid veil.

I joined my uncle at the church and cried, 'Please help me. I don't want to do this!'

'There, there,' he said, 'you've just got cold feet.'

My new husband was drunk most of the time and angry. His temper frightened me. I tried rationalizing it, but my body, particularly my gut, spasmed.

So that was fear and my intuition trying to attract my attention.

Of course, I knew I was not safe, yet I felt a primal desire to be with him. I had the feeling that his fearsome anger would be my protection.

It was not.

The beatings and emotional abuse began early in our marriage. I hid my bruises by hiding myself from everyone.

When he turned his anger on our sick infant son and five-year-old daughter, I lost my temper, jammed a .22 rifle in his belly, and threatened to shoot him.

With that final encounter, I took my children and fled.

The thing is, I knew it would happen this way, and

NO ONE LISTENED, including me."

Even if we can hear our intuition, we are shamed into silence, held to false standards, force-marched through a symphony of "shoulds," and ridiculed each time our dreaded, embarrassing intuition rears its head.

Unable or unwilling to hear our intuition, we are at the mercy of a manipulative, crazy-maker. Defenseless, we marry narcissists in blind trust and are inevitably betrayed and discarded by them.

Lori's story unfolds in just a few lines—*"I almost gave up my third child trying to save my marriage. My husband was already in another woman's bed as he brought me flowers and begged me to let him stay, only to change his mind repeatedly."*

From my talk with Queen Bee, Pamela Vatrano Kirastoulas—*"I was in love. At least, I thought it was love. I ignored the signs that something felt 'off.' And when I noticed him watching my every move, I thought it was because he was so into me.*

Then, one evening he said he'd call at a specific time. No call. I told him I was disappointed and asked what had happened. He brushed away my feelings with, 'It's not a big deal.' I let it pass, as usual. I didn't want to rock the boat. Maybe it was just me.

My friends didn't see a problem, "Are you crazy? He's gorgeous, has money, and buys you things."

That was only the beginning. 'Maybe it was just me,' I said to myself, again and again. Little did I know it was all an effort to manipulate and control me.

One day I broke free. Since then, I have learned to listen to my intuition."

Coping Is Not a Cure

Have you employed various coping skills? Does one of them involve a lifetime of shutting down to survive?

In the manuscript for her book Humble Pie, my client Sally Hendrick writes—"*I didn't speak until I was 12. I just watched.*

But I saw everything."

Yvonne says—"*I tried to stay invisible, which is difficult to do when you're a target.*"

And all you asked for was permission to live.

Revelation

Witness the natural voice of intuitive wisdom from Daisy Ting Du, spiritual teacher and forthcoming author. She emigrated from China, became a citizen, and then served in the US Navy. She models the perspective of intuitive understanding.

"*Mom was born into a hard life. She has loved learning since she was a little girl; however, harsh circumstances forced her to quit middle school to help support her big family of seven: parents, brother, and three younger sisters.*

Making four seasons of clothing and cooking, she managed every family chore. She always thought she was not smart enough, yet she could make all sorts of knitting works, sweaters, sweatpants, wool hats, and mittens for the whole family.

Her Chinese zodiac sign is Horse. So her life today is like a busy, warm-blooded horse supporting the entire family's smooth running.

Although she seems amiable in front of others, she often hides her unhappiness, nagging her life stories only to me. At least, that was how it appeared.

She complained a lot. That could be a way for her to process her years of sorrowful life and the compounded life stories, which she hasn't found a way to process.

I often felt claustrophobic and burdened when I was handed her tumultuous emotions and stories. I wished she would stop indulging in petty things, incessantly entertaining others' life stories and karmic loops. Maybe it was my delusion to assume she was unhappy. I always wanted her to do things like I wanted or face life in certain ways.

Maybe in a very similar way, everyone in her life wanted to direct or monitor her: siblings, parents, friends, colleagues, and random strangers passing through her life. She openly and vulnerably shared every piece of her life stories, letting others judge her and tell her how she should live.

Therefore, every single snapshot of her life story is filled with others' perspectives, flavors, likes, and dislikes. She took them all in, non-judgmentally incorporating everybody's judgments toward her and the hurts, pains, cuts, and scars from every single angle, corner, and walk of her whole life, up and down levels, and from different casts of society.

She never misses any person's opinions toward her. On the contrary, she patiently and willingly takes them all in as if devouring a big pot of delicious soup.

Often, she gets indigestion and can't figure out a way to fully integrate all the energetic imprints within her body. So she tosses and turns night after night, regurgitating, reliving, and reintegrating everyone's joys, sorrows, bitterness, and sweetness from all the visceral responses she harvested and harbored within her belly for decades, inundated like a gigantic memory bank porting centuries of emotional memory imprints for Gaia Mama Earth.

I wish I could find a way to help her digest or dilute the disharmonious edges of all the discombobulated emotions she has impregnated within herself. But *the older I become, the more I realize how important her role has been for everyone surrounding her.*

She's the buffer zone, the safe harbor, the anchoring ground for every soul in her life. In her own organic, simpleminded way, she unconditionally and abundantly opened herself up, letting others take a short layover in her little inner home, a nourishing oasis for all hearts.

'Take a sip of tea, drink, and patiently listen to all others' stories unfolding,' she says, patiently listening, observing, healing, and walking all lonely lost souls home through time and space."

Daisy's story is a revelation, a powerful example of how "listening" helps us understand. Instead of resenting her mother, Daisy's intuition helps her embody the soul connection that honors her mother's true nature and sacrifices.

Cloudy With a Chance of Awakening

The birth cycle of feminine intuition is a journey that each woman must take in her way and at her pace. It's not always a linear process, and various factors, including trauma, abuse, financial dependence, and PTSD, can influence it.

Have you ever felt like your life experiences have caused you to lose touch with who you are? Understandably, feeling disconnected from your inner guidance and intuition can lead to negative patterns of emotion like depression, hopelessness, and anger. I'm not a physician or a scientist, but my intuition brought me here to help you restore your ancient magic and intuitive inner balance. By doing so, you'll be able to live your life to the fullest and express yourself authentically.

So Where Do We Find Ourselves?

If your intuition guides you well, continue nurturing that connection through meditation, journaling, and spending time in nature. By staying attuned to your intuition, you can make more aligned choices and live a more fulfilling life.

If your intuition is not readily available, it is a sign that you must make time to restore yourself.

The Miracle of Restoration

It is not too late to receive the nurturing you needed from the beginning of your life! The following psychoactive journey is designed to embody your connection with **The First Mother**.

Prepare: Create some quiet, safe space to perform the restoration embodiment below. **This journey will download the memory of the loving guidance you <u>never received</u>.**

Adjust the ages you see mentioned to fit your experience. You'll see what I mean. Now read aloud:

"It is a sunny day, hours before my conception. Aunties, mothers, and grandmothers follow their Intuition to gather in a sacred circle and call my soul into this world. My consciousness responds with joy.

~

Time passes. Attracted by the light and promise of these diverse and beautiful souls, I am born into my little body and these women's lives. They celebrate my gifts of wisdom, intuition, power, creative expression, and happiness.

~

My auntie is teaching me to breathe deeply into my round belly. She says my belly is a strong, safe place to feel what I feel. So I exhale completely, inviting every part of my body to feel strong and secure.

~

Time passes. One day while making bread, my mother teaches me to ride the rhythms of life. Her voice merges with mine. We knead bread and sing the Hebrides Women's "Waulking Song" in rhythm—soft, sure, centered in power.

~

Time passes. One night, while getting ready for bed, I feel my heartbeat, and I'm worried I might die or that Mother may die and leave me all alone. "Oh, that won't happen for many years," she assures. "By then, you will have learned to listen to your intuition and walk in wisdom along your path."

~

Time passes. I imagine her arms wrapped tightly around me now as I melt into the depths of her love.

~

Time passes. I find I am forty-seven years old. The voice of The First Mother affirms that I am a whole and sovereign Being designed to speak my Truth and to be right where I am and in the flow. I am centered: wise, intuitive, curious, energetic, and sovereign.

I know I am beloved.

Guided from within—she is in me as the voice inside myself.

Indeed I am **The First Mother.**

This is the love that heals all wounds and thoughtless affronts. This love lifts you when you fall, soothes you when you suffer, and becomes **the voice** of what to do next and then what to do after that.

Thank you for joining me to Embody your Intuition.

Record this restoration journey and play it for yourself daily until you can feel it in your body.

Now

Embodying your intuition is about connecting with your inner voice and trusting it to guide you. It requires letting go of the limitations and mistaken beliefs passed down to you by your ancestors and society. Instead, intuitively create your reality to pursue your dreams and passions.

In my talk with Zita, she said—*"I learned to rely on myself for nurturing and information from a different source, the one 'inside.'"*

Your Intuitive Maintenance Plan

1. Start by taking time to connect with yourself.
2. Set aside time daily to meditate, journal, or do any activity that helps you connect within.
3. Notice your thoughts and feelings, and trust your gut (or your preferred talking body part) instincts. [repeat]
4. Question beliefs and limitations.
5. Ask yourself if these beliefs are serving you or holding you back. If they are holding you back, let them go to create new views that align with your intuition.
6. Finally, pursue your dreams and passions with courage and confidence. Trust that your intuition will guide you on your path and that you have the power to create the life you want.

Ha Ha! Yes, You Can Upgrade

After working with intuitive teachers, healers, and creatives for many years, here's what I know:

1. A new world opens up when we tap into intuition for **creative guidance**.
2. Our experiences form our lives, to be sure. **But sharing our stories transforms us and points the way for others!**

Here's the upgrade: You were born with potent inner resources. So after you hear and feel your intuition, remember to embody and express it in the world. Ask yourself how you would like to weave your gifts, thoughts, and feelings into creative expressions.

Write a book, blog, poem, or essay, or start a beautiful business that serves others!

Now Take the Pledge

- I Embody My Intuition.
- I feel, and listen to my Intuition, then take Right Action.
- When I would rather fall silent, I speak Truth.
- I create a safer space for myself and my community.
- My Embodied Intuition expands All Consciousness.

In conclusion, Embodied Intuition makes the connection between yourself and the journey to create a life that aligns your deepest desires with your highest purpose.

In the End, The Beginning—Honoring my maternal ancestry, I commemorate you and yours.

Judy Arleen McNutt, b. 1951 Santa Monica, CA

Daughter of Betty Darlene Donaldson, b. 1933 Grand Rapids, MN—d. 2012, age 79, Sedona, AZ.

Daughter of Adelaide Laura Litchke, b. 1900 Grand Rapids, MN—d. 1969, age 69, Riverside, CA.

Daughter of Laura Alice Jackson, b. 1861 Burnt Prairie, IL—d. 1926, age 65, Grand Rapids, MN.

Daughter of Mary J. Vaughan, b. 1823 Maury, TN—d. 1878, age 55, Fairfield, IL.

Daughter of Mary Elizabeth Hogan Walk, b. 1797 Maury County TN—d. 1870, age 73, Wayne County, IL.

Daughter of Sarah Paveley, b. 1769 Sawbridgeworth, Hertfordshire, England—d. 1830, age 61, Davidson, TN.

Daughter of Amy Hunsdon, b. 1732 Glatton, Huntingdonshire, England—d. 1790, age 58, Sawbridgeworth, Hertfordshire, England.

Daughter of Mary Read, b. 1695 Thorley, Hertfordshire, England—d. 1717 age 22, Thorley, Hertfordshire, England.

Daughter of Elizabeth Turner, b. 1670 in Essex, England—d. 1750 at age 80, Essex, England

pas de deux

It took years, but I learned about embodiment from the creator of Feminine Mastery, Cyndie Silbert, author of *True Calling- Awaken the Power of your true self.*

"DING! I feel it now, Cyndie!"

About the Author

Judy's journey to fulfillment begins when she embraces Cyndie Silbert's Feminine Mastery in 2015. As a Dragonfly-Hummingbird Archetype, she embodies the Honeybee, Butterfly, and Chameleon to offer holistic book coaching from her soul's gifts. With artistry, she blends skills and insight into the experience of teaching shiny-faced tiny humans in public schools, marketing and imaging award-winning radio stations, writing and publishing, and her practical energy practices!

Intuitive teachers, healers, and creatives need extra TLC to birth a book. Yes, their families and future readers need them, and overwhelm is not helpful. So she designs and trademarks a step-by-step system for book building for busy people.

"Writing and publishing a book is a magical and rewarding experience, even if you don't believe you are a writer," Judy says, and she created a quiz to help women like you find the place to start writing the book their intuition calls them to write.

Quiz: https://www.judymcnutt.com/writer-quiz
Waulking Song: https://www.youtube.com/watch?v=WzypgEbymC4
Email: connect@judymcnutt.com

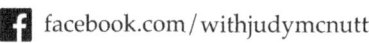 facebook.com/withjudymcnutt

EIGHT

Natalie Murray

DARE TO BECOME A 'FULLY EVOLVED' WOMAN

*I*magine there's an enormous, ethereal whiteboard in the sky above you filled with thick, black, messy writing. Those words record the fears, hurts, and trauma that have impacted you, and all the women who came before you.

You commit to the sacred healing, and then, astonishingly, one day you notice that not only have the words disappeared, but, in fact, the entire whiteboard has vanished, and all you are left with is YOU.

Present in this moment.

Breathing deeply.

No past defining you.

No fears restricting you.

No emptiness inside left to fill.

Like a butterfly freed from its cocoon after an exhausting, painful struggle, you now have a choice about how you experience the precious time you have left to live.

That's the miracle that's happened for me, and I want that miracle for you too, my love.

This feeling can only be described as 'Fully Evolved'.

There's such ease in knowing who I am, trusting I can handle any challenge, and not holding myself back for fear of what other people think.

It's an experience I could only dream of after decades of working on myself hoping to simply 'Love Myself, Be Myself, and Be Happy'.

Yet sadly, I know many female seekers never make it fully out of their suffocating cocoon.

They simply don't know it's possible to break out completely, they don't know how to do it, or they unknowingly sabotage the process because their deepest fears of not being safe hold them back *(and they don't even know it)*.

So, they settle, numb out, keep busy, deny their discomfort, squash their desires, and blame their unfulfillment on their past, their parents, their families, or their partners.

Until one day, they just can't take it anymore.

Something painful forces them to WAKE UP!

Their heart, body, and soul scream for them to listen, and to never give up on themselves.

They're DONE. OVER IT. KAPUT!

And now begins a search for escape from the constriction of their comfort zone they now realise is a self-created prison.

After decades of personal development and helping others heal, I too was unaware that I was stuck halfway out of the cocoon of my conditioning. I thought I was empowered, but I tolerated inner struggles thinking they were 'normal', still believed I had to work hard to fulfill my purpose, and dishonoured my boundaries even though I taught boundaries to other women!

Thankfully the universe delivered a series of 'wake-up' calls I had no choice but to heed, and, by becoming humble through this process, I owned I'd unconsciously been holding MYSELF back, took responsibility to live fully expressed, and transformed my entire life.

Without this forced awakening I never would have Fully Evolved, so here I share my heroine's journey, highlighting the deepest, darkest issues I had to face and transcend (as do many other women); describe what being Fully Evolved means and how to experience it; and invite you to take a first step if you too choose to Fully Evolve now.

My Awakening Story

Chapter 1: Living in an Illusion

It used to matter to me to do everything to the best of my ability and not waste my brains and talents by being selfish and lazy.

My work ethic was strong, and I pushed hard to do my best in whatever job I had. By my forties, I was burnt-out but didn't see it as 'burnout'. I labelled it as failure. I thought I was weak, and my mind obsessively tried to work out what was wrong with me. Why couldn't I cope like other women seemed to do?

I blamed my employer for not creating a supportive work environment, so I left that job to find another workplace that better suited me.

However, it didn't take long in my new job to burnout a second time.

It was humiliating, so I isolated and comforted myself with binge-eating.

Then I decided the only way to resolve my exhaustion was to become my own boss so I could use all my gifts, freely express myself, and determine my own hours and workload.

So, I reinvented myself as a solopreneur, helping other women empower themselves, but never imagined what a difficult journey lay ahead of me!

Chapter 2: The Realisation MY Way Doesn't Work

In true form, I threw myself into learning, signing up to a zillion courses, seminars, and free resources, and chasing every shiny bright object that promised an easy solution to build a successful business.

I believed if I just tried harder and gave more of myself then I could 'make my business work', but I quickly became frustrated, unhappy, and resentful.

Most of my business strategies didn't work, and my husband kept telling me to slow down, be gentle with myself, and to use the feminine embodiment tools I already knew and taught (but didn't practice) which annoyed the hell out of me!

However, after more failures than successes, I realised that my approach to growing a business wasn't sustainable, so I needed to do something different.

Chapter 3: The Awakening of Another Way

Seeking answers, I googled 'Feminine Empowerment' and discovered Cyndie Loven Fullenkamp's (nee Silbert) 'Feminine Mastery' empowerment framework that drew me like a magnet.

It felt like a big, scary stretch for me to ask for another woman's help, but the pain inside, and burning desire to live my purpose, motivated me to be vulnerable.

Cyndie helped me see my true calling (according to her 5 Part Feminine Mastery Archetype system) was to lead with a 'Hummingbird' Archetype (heart and throat energy), which meant I am here to inspire others to live openheartedly and speak their truth with love.

To be honest, this terrified me!

I was embarrassed to realise that, despite all the 'work I'd done on myself', I still didn't feel safe to be 'seen', my heart was still closed, and I wasn't 'grounded' in who I really am.

I really wanted to trust there was a feminine 'inner way' of succeeding in life, business, and relationships, but my masculine ego strongly resisted letting go of control.

Chapter 4: The Descent to Rock Bottom

Soon, I was heading for another burn-out.

It felt like there was a ten-tonne energetic weight on me, I became weak, could not think straight, everything I did felt hard, and I lost all my joy.

Denying the signs, I pushed on. But, over a period of eighteen months, the universe sent me a series of wake-up calls.

First, I contracted acute bacterial pneumonia that nearly cost me my life. My doctor was amazed I survived and said I was one of the strongest patients he'd ever had. And I felt sad because I knew on some level that being 'strong' was my Achilles Heel!

In true form, I tried to go back to work after a short rest and hired yet another coach, but then my beloved twenty-six-year-old niece, Rachel, died suddenly and tragically, leaving behind her baby and devastated family.

I felt guilty because I'd seen Rachel pushing herself hard in her business, and becoming unhappy, but I hadn't said anything, probably because on some level I knew I was doing the same to myself yet was too prideful to admit it.

Again, I took some time to grieve and then tried to work again, but one morning I was walking alone on a beach and the body of a dead, naked man, was dumped by the waves at my feet!

I realised the outgoing tide was pulling him out to sea, so I held on to him for twenty minutes before help arrived. Exhausted and traumatised, I again needed time out to heal.

By now I was exasperated by all the 'roadblocks' and questioned the universe, *'Why Me?'*

In reply I heard, *'Nat, honey, I'm trying to show you that it's time for YOU to die to your old ways completely'*.

Chapter 5: The Chance That Ended Everything

Ha! I so wish I could tell you I listened to that message and STOPPED, but you know I didn't, right? Oh, and by the way, it's ok if you feel like you want to reach out and slap me right now!

Yep! My prideful ego once again convinced me that if I just tried yet ANOTHER strategy THEN I could finally succeed in my business.

So, I hired an expensive writing coach with the hope of creating amazing copy that would attract my dream clients.

However, within a few weeks, I could no longer think or move. I was diagnosed with severe blood pressure, chronic anaemia, morbid obesity, and a frozen right hip, and I had aches and pains all over my body.

I had no choice but to finally concede I was burnt-out for a third time, that it was much worse than ever before, and that it was MY pattern and entirely my fault.

So, I did one of the hardest things I've ever done and walked away from my coaching contract with nothing to show for it and no money back. Although my ego was defeated, I finally learnt the biggest lesson of my life:

My health, happiness, and wellbeing are infinitely more important than money, success, achievement, making a difference, or living my purpose.

Chapter 6: The Death of My Ego

Left with no other choice, I graciously surrendered control of my life.

Not knowing or caring if I would ever make a comeback, I put strict self-care boundaries in place by closing my business, going off social media, and only giving energy to my recovery.

For five months I lay in bed because that's all I could do. In the stillness and silence, I became aware of the worried thoughts of my ego, *'What if people forget me? What if I have no value because I'm not "doing" anything?'*

Coincidently, that was the time in Australia when we entered an extended COVID-19 lockdown, and I knew in my soul I couldn't accept the vaccine.

Very quickly I felt the deathly grip of my deepest fear of being rejected by others for not 'fitting in', of being kicked out of the tribe, and being left to die alone. It sounds dramatic, but that excruciating fear helped me see that, despite my heightened self-awareness, I had still unconsciously been living my life trying to prove myself and please others to earn love. After years of therapy, I had 'known' that I was prone to doing that, but I'd resisted acknowledging how deep that habitual pattern ran in me and how addicted I still was to external validation, stress, food, staying busy, and social media to numb out and suppress my true self.

I also humbly admitted I'd dishonoured my body my whole life, had been stuck in blaming and complaining and seeking a 'quick fix' or 'magic solution' to growth and had resisted growing up and taking responsibility for my health, happiness, and results.

I'd reached a turning point and had to make a choice: play the victim card again, label myself a broken failure, and give up on my dreams OR graciously forgive myself, heal myself at a deeper level than ever before, and evolve into the woman of integrity I knew I could be.

My heart and soul chose the latter.

Chapter 7: Reaching Out and Birthing My True Self

First, I did something different and, instead of pridefully healing alone, I reached out for guidance and support and finally recognised how much power my self-destructive mind and ego had had over me.

Like a child learning to walk, I retaught myself how to be guided by my soul instead.

For example, before every move I make, I ask myself one of three questions:

1. Do I truly want to do this, or do I think I 'should'?
2. Will this choice honour me or dishonour me?

OR

3. What would I do now if I wasn't afraid?

It was scary at first to live life in a feminine way, at a slow and patient pace, trusting my gut, following my joy, and not making any concrete plans. But my happiness and energy started to return, and I was successful in my gentle efforts to replace bad habits with good ones.

I returned to Cyndie's Feminine Mastery Archetypes and called on my Butterfly sacral energy to help me honour my body, my Chameleon root energy to help ground me, and my Honeybee solar plexus energy to help connect me with truly like-minded souls and awaken my natural creativity.

Importantly, I also learnt that my purpose was not something I 'did' but the essence I shared with the world, which is of a visionary woman who embodies grace. And I discovered that my Life's Work is to use my healthy ego to sell something I love–which, in essence, turns out to be peace within yourself and your relationships.

The bottom line was, I'd exhausted myself by being a victim to my ego and my fear of not being safe to be the REAL me, and that fear wasn't even mine. It was ancestral, and even a collective consciousness fear, that I was born carrying in the very cells of my being. Thankfully, the cutting-edge, female-specific, trauma healing tool (called Creatrix®) that I use to help clients resolve their chronic, resistant issues quickly, helped me resolve my deepest-rooted victim imprint for good, without reliving any trauma, and saved me a lifetime of suffering trying to break the cycle!

Chapter 8: Free to Fly

In just two years I took my power back in every way, healed my chronic pain and health issues without medical intervention, stopped all 'numbing out' behaviours, and released the last of fifty pounds in extra weight the 'real me' had been hiding beneath forever.

All my relationships deepened after putting my wellbeing first, and I feel liberated KNOWING my insides match my outsides and I'm truly 'walking my talk'.

Sadly, my beloved mentor, Cyndie, passed in 2022, though I'm blessed she influenced me to BECOME the Hummingbird I was born to be, embodying unconditional love for myself and others, boldly speaking my truth, and creating a ripple effect of peace through my community and beyond.

The Essence of a 'Fully Evolved Woman'

Today I guide proactive, soulful female leaders, who also desire peace in their heart and their relationships, but, despite all the inner work they've done, still struggle to relax, be themselves, and be happy in relationships.

They're angry with themselves for still giving their power away by people-pleasing, taking everything personally, and letting people disrespect their boundaries and push their buttons.

They're frustrated about being emotionally reactive and habitually feeling like a victim, even though they know better, and are confused about how to break their repetitive relationship sabotage patterns.

I help them to humbly acknowledge, own, and resolve their deepest-rooted triggers and issues quickly at the core, master sovereign boundaries, and honour who they really are, so they can naturally express themselves, graciously stand in their power, and miraculously transform their relationships from disconnected to close.

By becoming wholehearted, their energy softens, and this inspires others to see, hear, and connect with them. Struggling relationships are healed, new relationships developed, and completed relationships ended with dignity and respect.

Some of the words my clients use to describe the essence of what it feels like to be a Fully Evolved Woman include:

Calm instead of anxious.

Confident instead of insecure.

Grounded instead of scattered.

Present instead of worried.

Vulnerable instead of guarded.

Strong instead of tough.

Feeling instead of numbing.

Real instead of fake.

Gracious instead of mean.

Allowing instead of forcing.

Expressing instead of suppressing.

Being love instead of seeking love.

Owning instead of blaming.

Responding instead of reacting.

Resolving instead of avoiding.

Connecting instead of controlling.

Choosing instead of pleasing.

Receiving instead of only giving.

When you land in this sacred place, no one can ever take it from you, my love.

It will become impossible to dishonour yourself or others.

And, although life and relationships will still throw you challenges, you will learn to embrace both pain and pleasure, re-open your heart, and keep moving forward.

How to Become a 'Fully Evolved Woman' Now

A profound, lasting transformation like this cannot take place until a woman is ready to claim her power to change and step into the next chapter of her evolution.

You see, in the first chapter of a healing journey, we're rightly focused on healing the pain that's been caused to us by our abusers, parents, families, partners, society, and the patriarchy.

But, if we only go this far, we risk getting stuck halfway in our cocoon, held back by unconscious victim conditioning, like I did.

To become whole and fully evolved, we must stop avoiding ourselves and look deep within to own our self-suffering, self-abuse, and self-suppression and take responsibility for how we hurt ourselves and our relationships.

As my story of healing my relationship with my health shows, it's usually not easy to see your own issues. You need someone like me to hold up an unconditionally loving mirror to help you see the gaps and hold you accountable to your transformation!

And here's what I know for sure—*when the longing whispers of your heart and soul become louder than the controlling voices of fears and ego, you WILL look.*

And, when you bravely see it, you can change it, even if it feels scary and you're afraid of letting go.

Dare to become a Fully Evolved Woman now?

I lovingly invite you to put your hands on your heart and call upon your Hummingbird Archetype to support you to take a next step out of your cocoon by arranging a complimentary, no-obligation meeting with me via my website.

Let's connect to see if we 'click', assess your challenges, and develop your path to become Fully Evolved too.

I can't wait to meet you and see you flying free!

Love,

Nat x

About the Author

Natalie Murray is an Advanced Female Empowerment Specialist who helps women shock and amaze themselves by how quickly they can uplevel their life and relationships.

Nat helps proactive, soulful, female leaders with past trauma who still struggle to relax, be themselves, and be happy in all relationships, despite the inner work they've already done. With Nat's guidance they finally resolve recurring, deeply rooted "issues", so they can freely be themselves, graciously stand in their power, and miraculously transform relationships from disconnected to close.

Restoring her wholeness after a traumatic past, Nat saved her struggling marriage, lost fifty pounds, became visible as a feminine leader, and earned recognition for truly "walking her talk."

Combining embodied wisdom, a mental health and trauma-recovery career, and uncanny gift for sensing what's blocking a woman's power, Nat offers an express, bespoke pathway, called *The EMERGE Experience*, which magically weaves together vital missing pieces of the feminine empowerment puzzle through 1:1 and intimate, online group programs.

At the core, Nat facilitates a little-known, cutting-edge, rapid, female-specific trauma resolution process that allows a female to safely heal and reset her own heart and nervous system back to their original design, and skyrocket her evolution, with irreversible results that can even be guaranteed.

Women who own that THEY are the common denominator in their relationship struggles seek Nat's gracious, direct guidance to shortcut their journey, so they can transcend their past, be grounded, present, and openhearted, and live true to themselves without the fear of being selfish or rejected holding them back.

www.nataliemurray.com.au

facebook.com/natalie.murray.3720
youtube.com/@nataliemurray1373

NINE

Micole Noble

BEING A FORCE FOR ENLIGHTENMENT AND CREATION: MY JOURNEY FROM DRAGONFLY TO HONEYBEE

*C*yndie Loven Fullenkamp, to whom this book you're reading is a tribute, fluttered into my life on a conference call in 2009. Only I joined her on the call; we considered it a wink from the Universe, a sort of cosmic 'set-up'.

Cyndie's voice came through the ether like an angel, though she could also speak truth to power. We giggled like schoolgirls, and I marveled as she led me to 'Clear, Connect & Create' what I truly wished for. She told it like it was and that grabbed my attention.

An author, mother, and my first mentor, Cyndie trained me as a Life Cultivation Coach shortly after that first heavenly encounter. Next up, workshops with Cyndie that I ate up as quickly as they were put down. I was on my way to my calling, which was to guide others to the truth of who they are. Transforming myself so I could guide others' evolution was what I was meant to DO.

Cyndie's two books: *Chameleon, Butterfly, Dragonfly* and *True Calling*, about the feminine archetypes deeply resonated with me. And when I was able, I attended the *Goddess Retreat* on the restorative island of Maui. The body of women that gathered seeking catharsis that week was pure **M A G I C .**

The Dragonfly archetype, "a messenger from the Goddess,"[1] was illuminated for me at this retreat. As I flitted about the world teaching, healing and guiding others using the Chopra teachings, it was awakening me to the truth of who I really am. Then, expressing my divine purpose was inspiring this realization in others. Embodying the Dragonfly expanded my capacity to speak, write, and model the way to others. Moving freely from one realm to the next, balancing my inner journey while helping others, I *became* that which I sought.

During the pandemic in 2020, Cyndie struggled as a parent (like the rest of us), and she seemed to be 'stuck' in both her body and her work. Life was happening, and I remember it as a painful time for many of us, both physically and creatively.

What magnificently assembled during this time was an online Artist's Way™ group, hosted by Cyndie and me. During the six-week course, Cyndie flew into action and swiftly manifested her dream home, or at least that's what it looked like. One minute she was vision boarding and the next purchasing beachfront property on the coast of Washington. Her Honeybee went into activity, from designing the building to picking out the finishes. Sadly, she never got to see this dream come to fruition.

Cyndie's cancer diagnosis came as a shock and only seven short months later she left this Earth. Losing my mentor and friend so quickly was a real blow, and the healing is a process, and that she is gone is still surreal to me.

Gone only from this worldly plane though. I feel her energy—in the hummingbirds, bumblebees, and butterflies— in *all* of nature. My guide and guardian angel, always by my side. Time keeps marching on, and the journey of life continues…from caregiving for my mother with dementia to surviving a six-month home renovation last summer. In gratitude for my daily routines that keep me grounded and connected to what's most important.

While Cyndie fought for her life, I remember having this thought: *What I really want is for my dear friend to live longer. And I want my mother to not live as long.*

The guilt for having this wish, of course, soon followed.

To Retreat Is Divine

Walking with a friend recently, I shared about my love of attending and hosting retreats.

"Everyone is healing from something right now…the pandemic, losing a loved one, caregiving for others, or just living the role of daughter, wife and Mom," I said.

"I've never been on a retreat," she confessed. "It always felt selfish to me to spend that kind of money on just *me*."

Her words both fascinated me and also made me feel guilty. Guilty because I live in a bubble, for sure.

It's actually not the norm for women to put themselves *first* and invest in themselves in this way. Therefore, many women have not experienced the clarity that comes from: (1) getting out of their current environment; (2) believing in a Universe that actually rewards them when they act as if who they are is enough; and (3) spending ample time in stillness and silence.

So, when did *retreating* become a thing? Well, turns out it goes back many centuries: "The retreat developed in the sixteenth-century Roman Catholic Church as a way of helping priests, other members of religious orders, and soon thereafter lay people to grow in their faith by way of an intense time spent in contemplation and meditation away from the day-to-day world."[2]

I reminisce about my very first retreat, in 2009, The Chopra Yoga Retreat. After years of listening to Deepak on my long commute, I finally decided to splurge. Admittedly, it took something to justify spending those dollars on just *myself*. The weekend was spent learning to meditate, practicing gentle yoga postures, and just chilling out.

The other best part of the retreat was weaving the Seven Spiritual Laws of Success™ into the yoga practice. It was immediately clear to me I would teach this—all of it—and I would teach it here, at the

Chopra Center, the premier provider of experiences, education, teacher training, and products that improve health and wellbeing. I was home.

Here's the point: if I hadn't invested in myself like this, I wouldn't have taken the first step toward my life's purpose. To take the leap and trust is priceless.

Money is energy. It is simply an exchange. If you want to be in business by yourself, you will surely need to put money into yourself. That's just how it works.

Time, too, is precious. However, we all have time and money for what is a priority.

Are you making YOU a priority? If not, why not? If not now, then when?

What are you teaching the children at home watching you stress out, play the martyr, and ultimately, resent them for all of it?

How's that working (or not) for you?

Now, this is not to say that just going to that one retreat was the answer to everything; it wasn't. A lot of things had to align, and they did, once I was clear on what I wanted to manifest. Most if not all of this journey called life is a process, not of learning new things but of letting things go. Letting things go is letting life flow. And to be in the flow is our intrinsic nature.

Activating the Honeybee

In addition to loving all things spiritual, I'm also a total nerd.

I want to know the science behind things, how things actually work. This has led me to try all kinds of experiments on myself and also to spend a lot of time and energy over the years trying to fix and change myself, make my life better, and find ways to be happier. Not a bad thing, but certainly something I'm releasing as I grow older and wiser. My intention for the future is to work smarter, not harder.

In 2010, I helped facilitate Cyndie's course du jour, fittingly called wOrth. We spent the weekend at a mansion in Rancho Santa Fe, eating healthy food and bonding with other like-minded women as we learned about ways to own our worth. A highlight of the weekend was a breathwork session, or holotropic breathing. It was close to three hours of what felt like hyperventilating that ended in a journey to higher consciousness and pure bliss. Since then, I've explored more of these types of classes, and each time I'm amazed at the layers of accumulated stress, pent-up emotions, and stored toxins that are released from my mind and body. Usually, I feel lighter, happier, healthier, and more authentically me.

The results of a breathwork practice are experiential, meaning it can be difficult to define and to promise what one will experience in a session. However, there is significant research and books about what breathwork actually does. Our breath, or *prana*, is our life force. We wouldn't be here without it, and if we treated each breath as the gift that it is, our lives would look very different.

That said, it's worth knowing how to breathe as our bodies were designed and how to use our breath to heal. My current obsession consists of a once per week trifecta: forty-minute breathwork, followed by forty-degree cold plunge and time in an infrared sauna to reset my mind, body, and spirit.

Another bonus: while transcending my mind just by focusing on my breath, I'm able to see what I want my life to look and *feel* like. Envisioning the future is as important as an action plan, if not more important. Like building a house, this vision is the foundation. See the view from the kitchen window and use these images as reminders of what you're doing the whole damn thing for when you find yourself in the trenches of the project.

While writing this chapter, in fact, I received a clear message from the Divine that my evolution as a Dragonfly—sharing the truth of who we are with the world—is expanding. It is now necessary to call on the Honeybee in order to innovate, up-level, and grow!

What this looks like is expanding my business by offering retreats in luxurious destinations around the world for others (and myself) to heal. I also cannot (and don't want to) create retreats in a silo. The Honeybee reminds us all that "her power is greater in numbers and that alone she can do very little."[3]

I'm now asking: *Who do I need to be in order to make this dream a reality?* And, not *how* but *who* can help me? To be truly innovative requires us to create "evolutionary advancement through the power of community."[4]

As I foresee my intended future, I *feel* it in my entire being. As I'm feeling, this frequency creates a vibration or resonance that the Universe then responds to: "Embodying your subconscious, conscious, and super conscious mind, the honeybee is the source of your creative power and innate ability to co-create with the Universe."[5]

Manifestation does not require us to have all of the answers. In fact, the details are the Universe's job. However, it *is* our business to:

1. keep the vision alive by acting as if it's already happened;
2. share our vision(s) through communication; and
3. detach from outcomes and trust that manifestations occur when the timing is right.

The time is ripe for breaking out of the ordinary in order to create the *extraordinary*.

When we are living the laws of the Universe, we are able to lead by example by serving ourselves and our families. When we do this, everyone and everything around us prospers.

Now, as the Honeybee, I am "spreading eternal optimism inspiring the masses to believe anything is possible through the practice of devotion and self-mastery."[6]

What We Feel, We Can Heal

Just as important as feeling into the future we want to create is transmuting emotions that are holding us back by identifying them during periods of transcendence, during meditation or as I spoke about earlier, by using our breath.

Many of us are healing from very deep wounds. Some things we are healing from are carried in our subconscious mind. This is what I mean when I say that what happens in breathwork sessions is difficult to describe. It's in the unseeable, the unknowable, that which is hidden from our view.

Think of a cell phone and the applications that may be open in the background slowing down the performance of the phone. Our minds and bodies are much the same. With awareness, we can begin to identify the old programming and replace it with new programming. Consider it 'upgrading' your current OS.

This is how quantum physics works. This used to sound woo-woo, like in the 1980s when Deepak Chopra and co-founder, Dr. David Simon, were teaching meditation to their patients and they were healing from cancer and other life-threatening diseases. Now, there is so much scientific data to support what ancient healers and sages have known for centuries. This is an integrative approach to health and wellbeing; using science *and* age-old rituals to heal.

By coming to a retreat, you will primarily be learning to meditate, breathe, and practice gentle yoga postures. It's during these spaces of stillness and silence that you will begin to do the work of self-discovery, to unravel some of the limiting beliefs, and let go of the programming that is no longer serving you.

It sounds simple, yes? It is. We humans are just really good at complicating things.

Lastly, you will form bonds with others at retreat as you contemplate your life's purpose and motives and then set intentions for your future. These connections are undeniably on purpose; by this I mean that those who join us on our journey to heal are not there by accident.

Several days of having a sacred space held for you is what leads to clarity, deep connection to Self and epiphanies galore.

'Self-discovery' is not just Self-ish, it is essential!

Return to Wholeness

The root word of health and healing is wholeness, or holy.

The journey back to ourselves, or 'self-discovery' as described in this chapter involves remembering the truth of who we are. Returning to wholeness is reuniting with ourselves.

Perhaps you've noticed yourself feeling fearful, confused, doubtful, or just plain numb about the future. Unfortunately, it's how a lot of people are feeling these days. In fact, depression is an epidemic not just in this country but also globally.

There's a reason, however, we feel a pull toward love, hope, peace, and calm. These are all qualities of the Self, or what is innate within us. With all that has gone on in the world, personally and collectively, we've picked up on the energy. An accumulation, over time, leads to dis-ease in the body, mind, and a feeling of disconnect at the level of spirit.

Rebalancing ourselves, then, has a ripple effect. Don't we owe it, not just to ourselves but to the world to shift consciousness on the planet? This has been my commitment and will continue to be. Won't you join me?

Reasons to Retreat

In case you're in need of more evidence to support the value of investing in a retreat, here are some of the benefits and why you should not feel guilty about taking this time for yourself:

1. **Reduce Stress.** Retreats are designed to be a break from your daily routine, allowing you to disconnect from the stressors of everyday life. This can help reduce stress levels and promote relaxation.

2. **Improve mindfulness.** Many retreats offer mindfulness practices such as meditation and yoga, which can help improve your ability to stay present in the moment and reduce anxiety.
3. **Gain clarity.** A retreat can provide a space for reflection and introspection, allowing you to gain clarity on your goals, values, and purpose.
4. **Connect with others.** Retreats offer a unique opportunity to connect with like-minded individuals, creating a sense of community and support.
5. **Boost creativity.** Removing yourself from your daily routine and immersing yourself in a new environment can help stimulate creativity and innovation.
6. **Enhance physical health.** Many retreats offer activities such as hiking, yoga, and healthy meals, which can promote physical health and wellbeing.

Attending a retreat is a valuable investment in your wellbeing, and you should not feel guilty about taking the time to prioritize your health and happiness. In fact, taking this time for yourself can ultimately make you more productive, focused, and fulfilled in all areas of your life.

"Practicing non-attachment empowers your vision and creates an expanded space for other like-minded people to join you."[7]

LET GO, and TRUST!

---

1. Silbert, Cindy. 2008. *Chameleon Butterfly Dragonfly*. Booksurge Publishing, p. xi.
2. "Retreat ." Contemporary American Religion. *Encyclopedia.com*. 12 Apr. 2023.
3. Silbert, Cindy. 2013. *True Calling: A Guided Journey to Your True Self*. North Charleston, SC: Createspace Independent Publishing Platform, p. 41.
4. Ibid., p. 41.
5. Ibid., p. 69.
6. Ibid., p. 40.
7. Ibid., p. 144.

About the Author

Chopra Global Mentor Coach, Transformational Leader, and Amazon #1 Best-Selling Author in *Sacred Spaces: Subtle Shifts for Mind, Body, and Home Transformation*

Since 2011, Micole has educated, coached, and mentored many in her work for Chopra Global, both in person and online. Sharing Vedic and life wisdom through coaching, writing, and continuing to experiment on herself allows her spiritual journey and path to healing to continue. A true devotion to travel and transformation has fueled her passion for creating sacred spaces to retreat in fabulous locales like Lumeria Maui Retreat Center, Carmel Valley Ranch Resort, and coming soon, Enchantment Resort Sedona.

In her chapter, Micole reveals her adventures with the Dragonfly as her archetype over the last decade to discover her own true nature. This experience has equipped her to lead others to do the same. Micole has received a clear message from the Divine to call in the Honeybee archetype to expand her hive, innovate to create what's next, and, of course, have fun along the way!

Micole has a heart-centered approach to everything she does and deeply listens to others with curiosity and joy. She facilitates the planting of seeds into the fertile ground of pure potential while detaching from outcomes. People experience becoming lighter, living more on purpose, and feeling more connected to themselves and those around them.

Micole is living the *Seven Spiritual Laws of Success*™ by giving to others while also expanding her own capacity to receive. She is an example for others to put themselves first so that they may have more to give to those they love the most.

Micole has a BS in communication from Cal State San Marcos and has three life coaching certifications. She is happily married to Todd, her high school sweetheart, and Mom to two amazing young men, Trevor and Gavin.

Website: https://micolenoble.com/

instagram.com/coachingwithmicole
linkedin.com/in/micolenoble

TEN

Kayleigh O'Keefe

THE QUEST FOR INTIMACY: FROM WORKER BEE TO QUEEN BEE

"Would you teach me how to do a cartwheel?"

I was thirty-two years old when I asked Pamela, a fellow author in this book, to show me how to do a cartwheel on the lush green lawn of Lumeria Retreat Center on the Hawaiian island of Maui. We were both attending a weeklong Feminine Mastery retreat led by Cyndie Loven Fullenkamp. I had been watching some of the other women on the retreat effortlessly flow through the long lawn cartwheel after cartwheel, back in touch with their childlike nature far from the mainland and any more "adult" concerns. I wanted to feel the full freedom in my body, too. My mind wanted to remind me, "You've NEVER been able to do a cartwheel. You're not a gymnast. You're a soccer player! You're not a young girl. If you don't know how to do a cartwheel by now, you will never be able to." The very fact that I asked Pamela for help was a sign that the magic of Maui was already working on me, that my independent self was easing into more vulnerability and openness to receive.

Pamela was delighted to help me! She watched my first attempt, which looked more like someone trying to pull off a breakdancing move. She offered guidance on where to focus my eyes and turn my body. I valued the specific feedback and kept trying. In just a few rounds, I found myself completing a fairly elegant cartwheel as I channeled my inner Dominique Moceanu, one of the American gymnastic stars at the 1996 Olympics who was seared into my psyche as a ten-year-old. I felt as giddy as a ten-year-old! And also so grateful for Pamela's attention, care, and support.

My roommate at the retreat was Natalie, also a fellow author here in *The Queen Bee*, and I felt her soulful, loving energy from the moment I crossed the threshold of our shared space for the week. At the time I couldn't name what I felt, just that I felt something in her presence. I would go on to receive some of her healing gifts as a client and, of course, we are now co-creating in this book. Micole and Stacie, two more women you will get to know in this book, were also on the retreat, and I found them both to be personable and vulnerable in a way that I wasn't used to yet at that time in my life and didn't realize I was absolutely craving.

Intimacy: The Most Valuable Currency

On one of the first days of the retreat, Cyndie gathered us in the yoga shala. I loved the ceremony and ritual of our arrival to any new gathering space on the property. Cyndie, and her co-creator and space-holder, Danielle, would give each of us undivided eye contact and a long full-body hug to welcome us into the space. I remember being so taken aback by the bright blueness of Cyndie's eyes and felt her see right through my tough corporate-woman exterior and into the playful, intuitive, creative heart that was yearning to be witnessed. I did feel seen.

In the yoga shala that day, Cyndie guided us through a heart-opening and grounding experience before inviting us to huddle closer together and around an easel. "What is your deepest desire?" she asked us. Without thinking, the first word that came to me was a word that I had never uttered before in my life. When it was my turn to add my desire to the board, I opened my mouth and shared:

INTIMACY.

I couldn't fully articulate at the time what I meant by this, but my whole body knew that intimacy is what I craved and longed for. I look back with so much admiration and love for that younger version of myself who spoke what was on her heart, and I appreciate her for bringing to my awareness the thing that I have since been dedicating my life to, sometimes implicitly and at other times explicitly: intimacy.

Intimacy, a deep familiarity, the sense of being witnessed, the feeling of being known—and still loved. I believe that so many of us are longing for true intimacy, starting with ourselves and extending out into all of our relationships. For many different reasons, we have lost a connection to our true selves and in doing so made it more difficult to create true connection with our fellow beings. Of course, at the core of the reasons for abandoning our personal desires and preferences have been protection, safety, and acceptance from our environment, whether you take that to mean the household you grew up in or the much broader culture you grew up in. So many of us called to the feminine awakening unknowingly divorced from our true nature long ago to earn love and seek approval. And so many of us who have witnessed what has happened to humanity as a whole over these last few years have begun to realize that intimacy—true connection—is the most valuable currency that exists on the planet and is the remedy to human suffering. Intimacy, care, witness. I believe our broken hearts are yearning for these salves for the soul.

It's no surprise that one week after returning from the island of Maui, more connected to my actual desires and not those that I thought I should have in order to win status and acceptance, I met a woman who I would propose to a year later. Prior to the retreat I had spent the last nine months exclusively dating men, determined to find a suitable father to my children. I really wasn't looking for a partner, I was looking for a father to hypothetical children!

After the most beautiful, intimate, and loving relationship with a woman, my first girlfriend and first real relationship ever, I abruptly ended things on the core belief that there was something "wrong" about two women raising children and that I "owed it" to any future children for them to know their biological father and to have a man in the house. Even though I knew within my being that I only desired to be in a relationship with women, I felt "righteous" and "good" to make the decision to sacrifice that part of myself in order to raise a family in the way that I thought "was better." And so, despite the beauty of our home life and all of its sweetness and intimacy housed in the little moments of French press coffees, Saturday evenings watching UFC fights and making roasted veggies, and cheering each other on at our soccer games, I left. I left my heart, body, and soul in pursuit of an illusion of safety, acceptance, and love. I am so grateful for my first girlfriend and how she supported me during that time, even as both of our hearts were breaking.

I pursued my goal of finding a husband with equal parts gusto and strategy. I laugh now at the realization that I was looking for a real-life sperm donor; how dehumanizing for me and the potential donor! And I'm really not kidding about the strategy piece, my friends. I got on the apps, I set up a Trello board for dating project management, I invested in new outfits and even a matchmaking service! I consulted with a friend weekly to refine my strategy. Some days I would search for dates in Dallas, Texas, a place where I figured I could find a strapping, wealthy man and, more importantly, be closer to my niece! Some days, I would turn my attention to Match and focus only on Catholic men; it felt dreamy at the time to imagine our perfect family in the Sunday pews.

On other weeks I'd stay local to the Bay Area and go on three dates a week with wealthy techies who were eager to show me their self-driving cars, home sound systems, and penthouse city views. Of course, the attention felt flattering, but that was all that I felt. I love getting to know people's stories, so I enjoyed the dates, but every first kiss left me wanting so much more, left me wanting what I had severed prematurely when I told myself I was wrong, that my desires were wrong, that my way of being was wrong. I swung so far from intimacy with myself that, in retrospect, it wasn't surprising that INTI-MACY was the word that popped for me when Cyndie asked us to share our deepest desires that day on retreat. Reconnected to my core on Maui, I felt safe again within to follow my heart, and instantly a new partner—who would earn the moniker "Rock of Love" the following year when we both returned to Maui for Feminine Mastery—entered my life.

The Evolution from Worker Bee to Honeybee to Queen Bee

The Productive Worker Bee

Have you prided yourself on being productive?

Have you valued yourself for being a giver?

Have you felt worthy by sacrificing yourself for other people?

If so, I would suggest that you, much like me, have been a "worker bee". That is, a highly attuned, empathic, and competent individual who works hard to uphold current systems in the world, albeit unknowingly. There is nothing inherently wrong with being productive, generous, and in service of others; however, for many of us on this path of awakening we've come to a point where we recognize that the energy behind these actions comes from a place of deep wounding, fear, or lack. This plays out like the daughter who harmonizes a broken household, the wife who "keeps the peace" among a dysfunctional family, sacrificing her own well-being to do so, or the woman who moves up the corporate ladder as a worker bee, feeling more performative and less heart-centered by the day.

Many of us worker bees have been working for the hive and specifically to uphold systems of lack and fear. Because we are so good at reading the room, knowing what is needed, and competently getting work done, we have often been manipulated by people in power, whether that person is a family member, boss, or political group. For me personally, this has looked like allowing myself to serve narcissists time and time again (until I realized what was really going on at a deeper, energetic level). I so deeply wanted to be seen and valued by narcissists (bosses or business coaches) at an unconscious level, looking to receive the validation or witnessing, rather, that had eluded me as a child.

The Inspired Honeybee

In the world of the divine feminine archetypes, the Honeybee archetype is the masterful creator: "A Honeybee creates from pure energy with evolutionary mastery. She works in service to a higher purpose by cultivating her gifts with the intention of becoming a contribution to humanity" (*True Calling*, page 184). When I made the decision to no longer use my gifts to serve the existing structures in the world (for me that looked like working in certain corporate environments), I took a bold step to transmute the worker bee into the honeybee. The honeybee is all about co-creation with the divine, and that is exactly what happened when I heeded the call to create Soul Excellence, my expression of leadership, and my invitation for people to co-create a new earth marked by a deeper appreciation for our shared humanity. The honeybee within me is the one that took the time to engage deeply with the practice of *The Artist's Way* and use the morning pages to listen to what was going on within me. The honeybee in me is the one who came up with book titles like *Leading Through the Pandemic: Unconventional Wisdom from Heartfelt Leaders, Significant Women: Leaders Reveal What Matters Most, The X-Factor: The Spiritual Secrets Behind Successful Executives & Entrepreneurs, The Great LeadHERship Awakening, The Diversity in Humanity*, and this very book, *The Queen Bee: Embody Your Truth and Live Fully Expressed*.

Each book represents me putting out a vision for the new world and inviting people who feel the same to share stories that weave this new vision together from our unique experiences and perspectives. I host a podcast called *The Future Is Human*, which is my honeybee transmitting an invitation out to the entire world to upgrade our human operating system by fine-tuning our emotional, psychic, spiritual, mental, and physical gifts. Thanks to Feminine Mastery and its founder, Cyndie, specifically, my honeybee has been fully alive and flitting about the world in intrigue and wonder and invitation!

The Sovereign Queen Bee

The invitation to myself—and perhaps to you, dear reader, right now—is to anchor in more fully to the vision for our kingdom. By anchoring to what is true, we elevate our honeybee into her fullest expression, The Queen Bee. Even as the honeybee, I felt myself often slipping back into old patterns and ways of being, specifically the long-followed protective mechanisms of people pleasing, taking myself out of the equation, silencing my voice to make sure everyone felt comfortable, and at times, ignoring my intuition. What would it mean for me to embody my truth and live fully expressed as The Queen Bee, as a sovereign, enthroned being from this moment forward?

As The Queen Bee, I am here to create a new kingdom, a new heaven on earth. I am for God, Universe, and I am for the men and women of this earth who are also engaged in the work of evolutionary mastery, that is the work of creating more intimacy with self, others, God, and the planet for the fullest expression of our shared humanity.

As The Queen Bee I am intimately connected to my mind, body, and soul, and I trust that my healing and return to wholeness has ripple effects around the globe. Since I have ultimate sovereignty, which is the precursor to true freedom, I am free to pivot toward my preferences, even when they seem like total departures from the path to the outside world. As the Queen Bee I joyfully create, share, and connect with those who are interested in creating new havens—new hives—for play, care, and thriving.

As The Queen Bee I deeply desire communication with my fellow bees! As a new solopreneur for the last three years and building a community-based publishing company from my apartment living room, I am craving, deeply craving, in-person connection and community with those like me who love nature, love learning, love observing, love expressing, love being in the flow with all of life. In isolation, this Queen Bee can easily lose her buzz and zest for life and succumb to feelings of loneliness and deep states of grief and depression.

In my kingdom, the principles are simple:

- Value intimacy
- Encourage play
- Champion creativity
- Hold space for witness
- Honor rituals
- Align on aspiration
- Live in multi-dimensionality
- Allow for the fullness of humanity

I want to invite you to join me, and so many women around the globe, who are ready and willing to see through the illusion of our current human reality and step into the truth and vision of this kingdom of heaven on earth, right here, right now. I am joining forces with my fellow humans who have truly woken up these last few years to see the extinction and suffering programs that are running the show and know, deep within, that none of it is serving us and we must, yes we must, become sovereign and stand FOR what we truly believe.

About the Author

Kayleigh O'Keefe walks the path of soulful excellence where she is a lifelong student and teacher of the inner way of leadership.

Sometimes referred to as a puppy for her endless energy, optimism, and playfulness, she is also quite serious about helping others to reconnect to their soul and pursue excellence on their terms. As the Founder and CEO of Soul Excellence Publishing, she holds space for strong leaders to let down their guard, write the next chapter in their life, and become bestselling authors along the way.

If you're into credentials, she's got that, too: a bachelor's from Duke, an M.B.A. from the University of San Francisco, and a former career advising Fortune 500 executives. Kayleigh is also a *USA Today* bestselling author, and as a boutique publisher, has published twelve bestselling books that have helped over 350 individuals become published authors. Kayleigh hosts *The Future is Human* podcast, a weekly exploration of how to upgrade our human operating system so that we can experience intimacy and connection.

Kayleigh loves being an aunt and brings "aunt energy" to all of her endeavors, pushing the limits of what's possible and what's expected. She is grateful that her niece and nephew introduced her to Disney's *Encanto*, and she won't stop singing it—at least not for another year or so! After spending most of her career in Washington, D.C. and San Francisco, she now lives and works by the beach in Ft. Lauderdale, FL, and is always up for travel!

Website: https://soulexcellence.com
Website: https://femininemastery.com/
Website: https://thefutureishumanpodcast.com/
Email: kayleigh@kayleighokeefe.com

instagram.com/KayleighOK_11
linkedin.com/in/kayleighokeefe

ELEVEN

Joy Paddison

FINDING JOY

The word courage is derived from Latin. The word 'cor' is Latin for heart.

'To speak one's mind by telling all one's heart'.

Therefore, to have courage is to live from your heart.

> *The wound is the place where the Light enters you.*
>
> —Rumi

This is my story.

Chapter 1: The Beginning

My childhood was unhappy, filled with anxiety and stress from living in the shadow of an abusive father trapped in his own suffering, oblivious to the pain he was causing his family, and a mother so shut down to her feelings I can only describe her as emotionally detached, a victim of her own childhood trauma.

The physical, mental, and emotional abuse from my father, a bully with a ferocious temper, forced me into a shell that I was too scared to come out of.

As a small child I was terrified of him, often screaming into my face from a few inches away, and accompanied by a hard smack, ear or nose pulling. Made worse with no other caregiver to offer comfort. It wasn't only his hand though, he also had a piece of wood and a cane, both of which I wasn't spared from.

To never be told I love you or given hugs was, to me, normal. I didn't know that for most families it wasn't. Daily verbal abuse included being called emotionally harmful words, such as moron, stupid twit, pest, galah, idiot, and foghorn.

"Shut up, foghorn," I was told when I was excited to share a story or just trying to be part of the family.

It was the one that I hated most.

My heart would shrink along with my voice, and I eventually became too scared to speak out, my voice locked in when I desperately needed it. I shut down to feeling the fear, and eventually my emotions were shoved deep down in the pit of my stomach.

And the thorns took root in my heart:

Family isn't safe.

Home isn't safe.

I don't remember when it first started, but the self-hate grew slowly over the years until I was numb to the pain and the depths of the hurt I was feeling.

I was fourteen when I started my daily mantra, *I hate you, I hate you, I hate you,* as I stared at my reflection in the mirror every morning, full of self-loathing after my sister told me that no one at school liked me. Our father's bullying had become a family pattern.

The bullied becomes the bully.

All the physical, mental, and emotional abuse tore my heart apart, leaving me unable to live in the world as a healthy functioning child, my feelings pushed so far down that I was numb.

I watched family shows on TV and wished I could swap. Spending time at a friend's house, I would pretend her family was mine. It was the only experience I had of what it felt like to be part of a real family.

I lived this way my entire childhood and carried it through my teens, playing out my emotional shutdown through alcohol, drugs, and other addictive habits.

None of which brought me the happiness I was desperately seeking, only more shame and guilt to pile on what I already owned.

This of course was a disastrous way to face the world, but I didn't know any better. The shame I felt for being so awful that my parents couldn't love me was overwhelming, and the only way I could live with myself was to drown it out.

The desperation of trying to fit in and be one of the cool kids was killing me. Both physically and emotionally, my soul was dying, and I couldn't do anything to stop the train of destruction I was on.

I lived for many years in this dark place, not wanting to own what I thought was the real me, not wanting to face the shadow in my heart that I knew was destroying me.

I had no way of knowing how to get out of my pain and turn my life around to have some meaning.

There was no one else to blame; it was my trauma that led me to the path I was on, one of self-destruction, loneliness, crying myself to sleep at night and the desperately lonely feeling of being alone in the world.

Nothing would change unless I made the decision to look at my emotions, to look at the pain I was causing to myself.

This was a lesson I would only learn the hard way, and I did an almighty job of that.

Chapter 2: The Middle

The Door

I close the door, I move the bed
My heart beats hard, the creeping dread
Will you come to steal my peace?
To satisfy your ugly beast
I lay awake, my ears alert
The fear you bring, the shame and hurt
My body chokes, it's gripping tight
The horror comes, the dark of night
Please go away, my silent scream
I beg to sleep, a silent dream
The angels cry, my heart it breaks
Your evil stench, my soul it takes
—*Joy Paddison*

I was sixteen when my bedroom door slowly opened in the middle of the night, rousing me from sleep. I opened my eyes to see a family member standing naked, about to enter my room.

I froze.

Summoning all my strength I could only manage to whisper, "What are you doing? Get out."

They backed away, but for the rest of the night I lay paralysed in fear.

My bedroom had always been a place of safety, one where I could escape, away from my father's temper and constant derision.

The next morning, I told my mother. She was still in bed and looked at me quizzically for a few seconds then closed her eyes; she didn't want to know. That was it.

I learnt then that I was on my own. I decided the only way to survive was to block it out and pretend it didn't happen, just like the abuse from my father.

Always numbing my feelings to survive.

Unfortunately, it didn't stop, and I lived in fear, hypervigilant.

Every night I would push my bed across the door to block the opening. This didn't stop them though, night after night brought the relentless knocking of the door hitting my bedhead, but eventually, they gave up.

Instead of retreating, the sickening actions escalated into other, more perverse behaviour.

It continued until eventually at the age of eighteen, I moved out.

And now another seed had been planted:

It's not safe to be a woman.

Unfortunately, this belief, along with all the trapped trauma from my childhood, had shut down my ability to suppress impulses in favour of more appropriate actions.

My emotions hadn't developed as they should, and I wasn't wired for cognitive control. My decisions were based purely on rewards and social acceptance.

I was now perfectly set up for the most destructive years of my life when I started looking for love in all the wrong places.

Pubs, music, drinking, and drugs.

I dove headfirst into relationships that were abusive and hurtful, three of which started and ended with sexual assault.

I was proving to myself repeatedly that I was unworthy, my feelings were not important, and I wasn't important, because that's what love is, isn't it? At least that was my belief, and it was all I knew.

Self-sabotage was my shadow, and I was dancing in the dark with everything I had.

All the shame and guilt that poured into my soul was not enough for me to stop. I knew in my heart my behaviour was wrong, but I didn't have the ability to self-regulate.

I tried to ignore the constant drip of self-loathing, but nothing worked.

Out of desperation, and in a decision that could have cost my life, I decided I needed control.

What I didn't know was that control has many dark shades, and when control came in the form of anorexia, I grabbed hold of it with both hands. It was my body that was the problem, so it was my body that would pay.

Anorexia is an ugly disease; it takes over your thoughts, your actions, your whole life.

Every second of the day is spent thinking about how little you can eat, how you can *not* eat, and what exercise you need to do to burn off the tiny morsel you did eat and the shame you felt for eating it. *If I can just get down to a certain weight, my life will change*, I thought, but the goal post always moved. *Just another kilo then I'll be safe*. It was a dangerous slope to be on, and I couldn't pull on the brakes.

I ended up at such a dangerously low weight that strangers were commenting in public, but I couldn't see it. I looked in the mirror and I still looked fat, I still wasn't happy, and I was still out of control. My family was oblivious. With every gram lost, I mistakenly believed the shame and guilt would go with it. I wasn't starving myself; I was letting go of trauma, at least that was what I believed.

The truth was it wasn't the trauma that I wanted to die; it was me.

I struggled with my daily war over food for about eighteen months until one day, and I remember it clearly, I was looking at the food on my plate, full of disgust with myself and fighting the urge to eat when I decided enough was enough.

I have no idea how, when, where, or why, but it was at that moment my enemy retreated. Retreated but never surrendered, and even though I had managed to loosen anorexia's grip all those years ago, to this day I am aware it's always lurking, waiting to pounce as soon as I start to feel the need for control. I didn't know just how out of touch I was with living a truly authentic life.

By this time, I believed getting married and starting a family would finally bring me the self-worth I craved. Then I would be whole and able to crush the shame and guilt once and for all.

Or so I thought.

Outwardly my life had changed, my husband and family were my focus, and our life was full of regular family stuff, working, school, games, and sport. I was determined to make sure our children grew up part of a 'family'.

As a traumatised child, you learn to pretend that you are ok, like an armour, a shield that will keep you safe, yet as an adult, I was still living within my walls and trapped inside my prison of self-loathing, and nothing it seemed was going to change that. It was me and I had to accept it.

Death
It's calling me
I hear my name
It's calling out
It screams my shame
The sound of death
I hear its claws
It moans my pain
The darkness calls
The voices shrill
A cruel request
Come quickly here
I'll give you rest
—*Joy Paddison*

Life went on and I tried so hard to live with my shame, but it was a losing battle, and eventually when I was fifty-two, I finally reached rock bottom, "If this is life, then I don't want it," I told my friend.

It was 2011 and I was deep in my dark night of the soul.

Chapter 3: A New Beginning

My friend looked at me with a warm look on her face and handed me a pamphlet for a centre in New South Wales, Australia, for survivors of childhood trauma and abuse.

I didn't know it would be the catalyst for change my soul was crying out for. It was to be the start of my incredible healing journey.

I had never been to any type of counselling or therapy before, and this was a live-in weeklong retreat. I knew instantly that I was going. I was nervous to tell my husband, but I was determined.

"My inner child is dead," I announced to the group when we were asked to explore in our hearts for our inner child. This is not uncommon for survivors of childhood trauma and abuse, and it is due to the crippling effects on an undeveloped brain. My inner child had completely shut down out of fear; home was not a safe place. I also learnt for the first time the ways in which the trauma I had experienced as a child and young adult had impacted my brain.

I had them all.

Trauma's Impact on the Brain

Exposure to chronic, prolonged traumatic experiences has the potential to alter children's brains, which may cause longer-term effects in areas such as the following:

- **Attachment:** Trouble with relationships, boundaries, empathy, and social isolation
- **Physical Health:** Impaired sensory motor development, coordination problems, increased medical problems, and somatic symptoms

- **Emotional Regulation:** Difficulty identifying or labelling feelings and communicating needs
- **Dissociation:** Altered states of consciousness, amnesia, impaired memory
- **Cognitive Ability:** Problems with focus, learning, processing new information, language development, planning, and orientation to time and space
- **Self-concept:** Lack of consistent sense of self, body image issues, low self-esteem, shame, and guilt
- **Behavioural Control:** Difficulty controlling impulses, oppositional behaviour, aggression, disrupted sleep and eating patterns, trauma re-enactment

(Source: Cook et al. 2005)

No wonder my life was a train wreck; it was a relief to learn there were ways to unwind the damage and allow the stunted emotional development to repair, self-care being number one.

The week was full of tears and joy, learning to find my voice and set boundaries, to finding my inner child. It was to be the start of my long healing journey; I was on my way to self-love.

Chapter 4: A Whole New World

"Awakening is a shift in consciousness in which thinking and awareness separate."

—Eckhart Tolle

I returned home from the centre, my heart full. I slipped back into my life but this time with a different awareness; I was now implementing the practices that I had been taught.

For the first time ever, I had hope.

I didn't know it at the time, but my life was about to change even more, when one day as I was cleaning out my old wallet, I came across a bestselling book review that I had cut out of a newspaper years before, in 2005.

It was Eckhart Tolle's magnificent *The Power of Now*, a book that would completely change my life.

Right then and there I ordered the book, not knowing that this would be the start of my spiritual journey; I didn't even know what a spiritual journey was. It turned out to be an incredible exploration of the metaphysical world and all the joys that exist outside the mind.

From then on, I was reading every book I could on spiritual-enlightenment. Anything that showed me that there was more to life than what I had experienced up until then, I devoured.

One day I was sitting in my armchair in our bedroom reading *Hidden Treasure* by Gangaji.

"I surrendered my ideas about life as well as most of my ideas about myself, and prayed for true understanding. I began the challenge of stopping work on my story" she wrote, *"Without knowing exactly how to surrender, I was willing to take the plunge. I was willing to stop telling my story, and I now invite you to stop telling yours"*

This sounded radical, but I was open to anything and everything. I put the book down, stood up and threw my hands in the air; *"OK universe it's all yours, I surrender,"* I said.

There were no lightning bolts or messages from the heavens, so I smiled to myself and went off to shower.

As I was standing under the water, lost in thought, a big empty space opened in my crown and a voice said, *"You are home now, Joy,"* and small white cards started flashing in front of my eyes. On them were written the words *"hate, anger, jealousy"* and many others. All negative beliefs that Gangaji wrote of in *The Diamond in your Pocket;* that *"only exist when linked to a story!"*. Then the voice said, *"These are all here, Joy, but they're not you."*

I finished showering and dressing, and walked around the house in a daze. My awareness was fully opened, I could 'see' the illusion, the dream, with no linear time or space. It was to be my 'spiritual awakening', and for the first time that I could remember, my heart was open.

I would love to say that from then on, my life was perfect, that I am now an 'enlightened being', but it isn't and I'm not. My spiritual journey is ongoing, and the usual trials and tribulations are still there to be dealt with, but I'm a mile further along than when I first told my friend I'd had enough.

Today I'm writing this in my office on our family farm, and I'm so grateful to be here and for all I've been through.

To anyone reading this who is losing or has lost hope, I want you to know there is a light at the end of the tunnel, the light is love, and it's waiting for you.

My healing journey has brought me to a place where I am able to walk in the light with confidence as my true authentic self.

I've discovered the power of 'true meditation' combined with the courage to set personal boundaries.

I know that **I am** the one who will save me, **I am** the one who will comfort and love me, **I am** the one responsible for my life, no one else.

I found the one I was searching for, I found myself.

I found Joy.

Finally, to my husband, Garry, my dedicated wingman throughout our forty years of marriage, I truly couldn't have done this without you. I love you.

Forgiveness
I forgive
I free myself
From all the pain
My soul has felt
I'm free to love
The whole of me
To live my life
To just be me
—*Joy Paddison*

About the Author

Having recently retired after selling the successful local agricultural business she owned with her husband Garry, to a global corporation, Joy Paddison started exploring life as a writer.

Now a published author, her children's book, *Milla and the Magic Springs*, was written for her granddaughter Milla, complete with fairies and talking animals, where anything seems possible.

And anything is possible is the message Joy brings in her chapter, "Finding Joy."

Guided to share her personal journey of moving from her dark night of the soul onto a path of self-discovery that led to healing the sacred wounds of her childhood, Joy was brought to a place in her heart that summoned all her courage, The courage to share her story of the shame and guilt she had stored locked away in her heart.

Describing the power of healing as a survivor of childhood trauma and abuse is an honest, heartfelt, personal story of the shame and guilt that trauma brings.

Joy shares her journey through learning about the effects of trauma on the brain, combined with her spiritual journey and how she was able to change her life.

Joy is honoured to be asked to contribute to *The Queen Bee* and has written her personal story to give hope to other survivors.

Now happily settled on a picturesque farm near Parkes, New South Wales, Australia, with her husband, Garry, and their loyal sheep dog, Joe, Joy has found the life she longed for as a child.

Connect with her via email:
joypaddison@icloud.com

TWELVE

Robin Toft

BECOMING LOVE IN ACTION

"There's an asteroid in your house of marriage," the seasoned astrologist told me nonchalantly while reading my star chart at the Canyon Ranch. She went on to say that she had never seen so much fire in a chart in her thirty years of giving personal readings. I was attending a wellness retreat in Tucson, Arizona with some girl-friends, attempting to relax and recover post-divorce. She added, "When you heal, you will be able to heal others." She also said, "Do you teach workshops? If not, you definitely should, because you have the potential to inspire many women." At the time, these predictions all seemed incredibly far-fetched given my twenty-six year marriage had imploded the prior year, and I was personally struggling more I was willing to admit.

At the time, I thought I'd bounce back quickly and be back to my old self in no time. I remember experiencing feelings of deep sadness and absolute aloneness. Cheering myself up, which had always been easy for me, became difficult. I spent a lot of time crying with my chocolate lab puppy, Rowdy, who had also experienced the loss. As a passionate career professional, I was living my purpose, wildly committed to my personal mission, and I was extremely independent. In truth, I had become harder to live with when I became Founder & CEO of my own company. And now I was experiencing what it was like to live alone with myself.

If you'd told me as a young girl that I would build a company dedicated to advancing women's careers in order to cure cancer, I wouldn't have believed you. If you were to add becoming a published author and inspirational speaker, it would have resonated a bit more with my younger self, but it would still require a huge leap of faith. It's clear in hindsight that the plan God had for me was so much bigger and more perfectly aligned to my strengths than I could have ever imagined once I learned to have faith and patience. My journey to my current definition of success included a series of tough lessons that taught me to take even bigger risks and experience the rewards of listening to the soul for guidance versus the ego.

In my youth, I actually already knew how to dream big and create space for information to come in. I often lay on the grass looking up at the clouds and envisioned how bright my future would be–I was manifesting it, but didn't know it at the time. My family and friends thought I was just a big dreamer, and quite erratic in my decision making at that. As an example, I could never explain why I needed to put it all in the red convertible and drive cross-country from the suburbs of Detroit to San Diego to pursue my dreams. I just naturally knew it....Now I know I was actually listening to my soul.

Once in San Diego, I met my future husband, and three months later we moved to Hawaii for his first big job offer. After living together for three years, we got married barefoot on the beach by a free-spirited Hawaiian minister. Six months later I was heartbroken when my husband decided we needed to move back to the mainland so he could pursue a future career as a wildlife photographer. Back in San Diego I quickly landed my first sales role, and I became the top performer in the company in my first year. Given my Midwestern work ethic, running on the sales treadmill from dawn to dusk was easy for me. I routinely slept only five hours per night, not realizing it was bad for my health. With my ego at the wheel, I became an over-achieving, sleepless workaholic for the first ten years of married life. My ego pursued this lifestyle as if it were all-important. I collected awards, corporate incentive trips, homes, and sports cars as tokens of my over-achievement. Underneath it all, I harbored a strong undercurrent of uneasiness, "not-enoughness", and dissatisfaction. Still, in spite of the sleepless nights, I carried on and continued to win awards and accolades. Society applauded my performance, and I numbed my lack of self-love with work.

I became very comfortable playing the role of the primary breadwinner within a loving marriage to an ambitious wildlife photographer. It was my story, and my customers and co-workers loved it. Soon, I began a hitting series of emotional speed bumps, which at the time I judged as inconvenient. While working hard as an executive in biotech, my father had a medical emergency and ended up in a coma and on a ventilator. I remember exactly where I was when I asked God for help, driving at top speed up a mountain on the way to the airport to catch a flight home. It was as if the skies had parted and S/he was there in all her glory answering my urgent cry for help. My father ultimately recovered and was able to finally receive treatment for his long-term depression, which had caused the accident to begin with. My prayers answered, I briefly registered the underlying message that health, love, and relationships are what life is really all about.

Several years later, I received another message from above which was impossible to ignore or override. I was flying to Europe for business, got sick on the plane, and ended up in the hospital myself. Surprisingly, I was diagnosed with colon cancer in the emergency room, and the "cure" was immediate surgery and six months of chemotherapy. I knew immediately that if I did not slow down significantly, my life was at stake. I resigned my executive role and moved back to San Diego to live remotely in nature on a mountain and consider how to move forward. In parallel, to further reinforce my need to focus on love, my beautiful white dog Kona was also diagnosed with cancer. We both went to chemotherapy together over many months, and I was reminded how beautiful and short life can be. I also realized I still had a lot more to give, since I hadn't made a big enough difference in the world yet, which became my focus for the rest of my life. Losing Kona way too soon reminded me again that love, health, and relationships are the foundations of a meaningful life.

As soon as I recovered from cancer, I returned to work with renewed urgency. I threw my energies into building an executive search company intended to change cancer care in my lifetime. In truth, I was still running on the treadmill, but now after a more meaningful goal. Having not changed my pattern of "action for love" vs. "love in action", the following year I received another loud message. While my husband and I were traveling out of the country on a much-needed vacation together, everything we owned literally went up in smoke. Our beautiful mountain retreat burned to the ground in the San Diego wildfires, and my husband and I both suffered emotionally. He was really hurting, having lost fifteen years of irreplaceable images. I had already learned the importance of love, health and relationships—the only things that truly matter in life. Over the next ten years he experienced several life-threatening illnesses, and then experienced his own cancer battle, for which I became his caregiver. He ultimately recovered and yet once again I realized my work was STILL taking a central role in my life in spite of it all.

Exactly ten years after the fire, when I was personally thriving as a CEO, having built a fun, mission-driven, people-first company where employees felt like family. Like the wildfire that took our home ten years before, I was completely unprepared when the love of my life told me he no longer wanted to be married. It honestly took me by surprise, although it shouldn't have. For our entire married life, my addiction to work had taken priority over my love for family, relationships, and my health. In spite of all of the warnings from my soul, my ego had been running the show. My ego convinced me I had no choice other than to work hard and continue to make as much money as possible, by leveraging the fear of losing it all. My soul, on the other hand, had been dissatisfied and discouraged for many years.

I had always known deep in my soul that happiness wasn't about the things, the money, or the accolades. Of course I enjoyed them all. As a married couple, we were living the dream, but we had no time to focus on building our relationship. In addition to founding and running my own company as CEO, I also served as the CEO of his photographic tour company. Our vacations had become joyless because one of us was always working. We both traveled so much for work that we had no energy left for travel and creating new experiences when we were home. So instead we hosted beautiful parties on our ocean view deck, including live bands, tons of friends and family, and dancing…always dancing! Our friends would have told you we were the happiest couple they knew, and I thought we were "happy enough". But when we really slowed down enough to reconnect, it was clear that we both missed the times when we were footloose and fancy free in Kauai thirty years ago. We reminisced about times before we had embarked on these careers, which had begun to take over our lives.

I've observed this same dynamic in many partnerships since then, and I believe it's a common one for many successful career women, like the men before them. As women are rapidly advancing in their careers into top jobs, their husbands are often expected to take the role of smiling, supportive spouse. At the same time, men are still programmed to be providers and are encouraged to take on traditionally male roles. When they earn less than their female counterparts, their self-esteem often suffers. In truth, I never expected this to happen to my husband who was not caught up in the pursuit of material things, but in the end I believe he simply didn't feel like I needed him, which became unbearable. Although I always prided myself on being present for him, I was busy! We had gradually lost what I now consider the three foundations of a successful partnership: communication, companionship, and finally our connection.

Before the asteroid landed in my house of marriage, I was blissfully naïve. I worshiped my wildlife photographer husband. I believed that marriage was for life, and life was supposed to be hard. There would be ups and downs, but we would get through it. The truth is that I would have done anything to have a different outcome, but it was too late. In that moment I lost my best friend, all of my belongings, my home, and essentially everything that I treasured. The message was so painful, loud and clear, that I had no choice other than to embark on the long hard path to recovery, awareness, and self-love.

My first reaction was to cry while baring my soul to Rowdy, my chocolate lab, for approximately six months. I remember one evening sitting at my kitchen counter in distress and feeling like I couldn't go on. So, for the first time in my life, I sought out a therapist—finally doing something for me. In our first insightful hour together, my therapist taught me the one significant truth: "people need what they need." With his traditional male programming, my partner's male ego " needed to be needed." So, the new question became, "What do I need?" Like so many female overachievers, I had never considered this, and I was completely uncomfortable putting my own needs first. I didn't know what it meant to love myself, and yet I was excited to start the journey.

I'm happy to share that the "recovery years" have been the best years of my life, and so many miracles have transpired since then that it is hard to count. Early in my recovery journey, I received a very specific message from above while trail walking with my dogs in nature. My soul suggested I hire a man I barely knew to lead operations of my organization so that I could continue my public work with female executives and philanthropy. He agreed to join the company as my partner and immediately shined a light on my workaholism, stating he clearly would not support it. Leading by example, he reinforced the importance of living with a strong spiritual center, unwavering commitment to God, and exceptionally strong family values. This gifted and talented man has since become my best friend and my mentor. We share a deep love for life and have both grown personally and professionally, while teaching each other how to be in a relationship that is both inspirational and edifying.

Next, I received a message from my soul that it was time to write my first book, *WE CAN: The Executive Woman's Guide to Career Advancement*. My goal was to teach women how to accelerate their career journey while partnering more successfully with men to build stronger companies. With impeccable timing, I miraculously met a woman who was a neighbor who had a publishing company and she helped me bring my book to life. *WE CAN* went on to win accolades as one of the top 100 CEO books of all time, and I won international acclaim for sharing my "headhunter perspective" on career development.

Taking my own advice, I then sought out a career coach to explore the intersection of my professional and personal lives. My goal at the time was to address my workaholic tendencies and to learn how to stay "in joy" all the time, not just on the weekends. Shortly thereafter, I happened to meet a talented artist who told me his wife was a career coach. I was not initially excited to be introduced to her because I've known a lot of career coaches, but Donna Bond was different. Having experienced a corporate career before becoming a coach, Donna was the perfect guide for my soul's continued journey. She laughs because the first time she met me I was completely energized and telling her about the awards my book had won and talking a mile a minute. She was absolutely certain I would never contact her as a student. Somehow my soul knew what it needed. I called Donna, and the recovery journey began in earnest.

While continuing my work with Donna, I identified several important lessons I needed to learn while in "earth school". My personal lesson plan included facing one of my biggest fears, navigating from "betrayal into trust," which had been a theme in my life. I realized that my divorce had caused significant collateral damage to my self-esteem and confidence and had destroyed my ability to love and trust not only other men, but more importantly myself. The journey to self-love and forgiveness was long, arduous, and worthwhile. I have learned to trust and fully love myself—my fully human, flawed, beautiful self. And the highlight of my recovery journey was when Donna officiated my self-love ceremony with four friends and my dogs as wedding guests on my sixtieth birthday. I've never felt happier or more loved than in that moment.

When the company I had founded reached the ten million dollars in revenue milestone, my soul clearly let me know that it was time to sell it, and to consider the next chapter of my career. With the help of my executive team and bankers and another miracle, I was able to efficiently transition the company to a new owner immediately before the pandemic of 2020. Having created and sold a company dedicated to changing cancer care and advancing women in the workplace is now a highlight of my professional career.

Today, I look back at my journey to joy and self-love with reverence and awe. On the path to awareness, my personal definition of success has evolved from one of ego-driven personal achievement to soul-directed "giving and receiving as much love as I can in my lifetime." I invite God into all of my relationships and pray for what I need, which I trust S/he will answer if it is for my best and highest good. I renew my faith in love versus fear daily. And most importantly, I have learned to trust and follow my soul's guidance while noticing the miracles along the way. I am excited to see God's plans for me unfold as I continue this journey called life, confident I'll be able ride the roller coaster with enthusiasm, joy, and love, hands in the air.

My Self-Commitment Vows – August 3, 2020:

On a "milestone" birthday during the 2020 pandemic, I decided to invite four close female friends to participate in a self-commitment ceremony at my home, with my dogs also joining the wedding party. It was a day to celebrate my journey to "self-love", and the commitment to become authentically me, a woman who lives in joy daily and makes every effort to be "love in action" vs. "action for love". These are the vows I wrote to myself, which have been my guiding principals in my recovery journey:

- I promise to remind myself each day that which I seek is actually inside of me—I am perfectly whole and unconditionally loved right now.
- I vow to accept myself completely just as I am, and to remember that I am always perfect in God's eyes.
- I promise to continue to prioritize my personal growth as I seek to deliver upon God's plan for me with my heart, body, mind, and spirit
- I promise to refrain from self-judgment and self-doubt, and to let my daily actions and future choices be firmly aligned with my highest purpose.

- I vow to walk hand in hand with God, with all my human limitations, natural beauty, and radiance, and to remember I am fully supported on my journey at all times.
- I vow to let go and let my soul show me the way each day, while listening carefully for divine guidance and prioritizing that voice above all others.
- I vow to listen to my soul and to receive divine guidance on all of my opportunities, reminding myself that I am always exactly where I need to be in each moment.
- I vow to honor myself always and to respect that each opportunity given to me is in fact for my best and highest good.
- I promise to be my own mirror and to allow myself to fall off my path without judgment and help myself to get back on.
- I promise to remember that in every minute there is an opportunity to be fully present and to be connected with my soul, in the form of my divine, authentic, lovable, glorious self.
- I vow to live a life filled with gratitude, generosity, and abundance while inspiring others to deeply love themselves and to respect their inner guidance as a message from their souls and their divine truth.

About the Author

Robin Toft is an inspirational leader and the award winning author of WE CAN: *The Executive Woman's Guide to Career Advancement*. Robin is committed to elevating women worldwide by educating companies on the competitive advantage of building inclusive leadership teams. WE CAN was recognized as one of the top 100 Best CEO Books of All Time by BookAuthority and provides the confidence, language, tools, and practical advice for women to design and realize the career of their dreams. Both WE CAN and her second book, *Ignite Your Board Career: Board IQ Playbook*, are available on Amazon.

Robin is renowned for building high-performing organizations by recruiting women and under-represented candidates into top roles and overcoming unconscious bias in hiring. She has served as Global Life Sciences & Boardroom Diversity Leader of the fastest growing global executive search firm ZRG Partners. Prior to joining ZRG Partners, Robin was Founder & CEO of Toft Group, an executive search firm focused on the placement of female executives in life sciences and healthcare high tech. Her company rapidly grew to over $10 Mio in revenue before Toft Group was successfully acquired by ZRG Partners in 2019. Prior to founding Toft Group, Robin served twenty years as a biotech executive. Robin currently serves on the multiple board of director roles for companies advancing women worldwide.

WE CAN is available in all formats: My Book

linkedin.com/in/robintoft

THIRTEEN

Pamela Vatrano Kirastoulis

TAPPING INTO YOUR DIVINE FEMININE BEAUTY

Divine Beauty

What is beauty? The world's definition is a combination of qualities, such as shape, color, and form that pleases the aesthetic senses, especially sight. You've heard the

expression, "a woman of great beauty." Perhaps someone comes to mind when you think of a

"women" and "beauty" in the same sentence.

Working with thousands of women over the past thirty-five years in the skin care and cosmetic industry, I have experienced all shapes, forms, ages, colors, and sizes of beauty. All looking to enhance, update, lift, smooth, and even change their look to meet their standard or the world's standard of outward beauty. I get it! There are products and procedures that can certainly promise glow, radiance, and age-defying effects. But I want to take you on a journey to a different kind of beauty. The kind of beauty that is within. The divine spiritual beauty that resides within each of us. In the Bible, God refers to true "beauty" as being a focus and cultivation of our inner spiritual qualities.

"Beauty should not come from outward adornment." Instead, "it should be that of your inner self, the unfading beauty of a gentle and quiet spirit, which is of great worth in God's sight" (1 Peter 3:3–4 NIV).

Broken Beauty

Do you know the story of Humpty Dumpty? He was sitting high on the wall, but then life came and he had a great fall. No one could put him back together again. Not the king's horses or his men. I wonder what happened to Humpty? Well, I can relate to Humpty. I was high on my wall of life. Living in a prominent neighborhood in a beautiful home with my husband and two daughters: healthy, happy, prospering, and loving life. I was in the country's top 20 sales leaders in my career as a director, leading a million dollar team in the beauty and cosmetic industry. I had built my own little kingdom and I was sitting on the throne, crowned as queen. And then, the FALL came. It started with a fallen marriage. After eighteen years together, our relationship had drifted apart. Next, financial devastation was unveiled, followed by a life-changing health scare.

Everything I knew that was holding me together had crashed into pieces. As I put the pieces back together for me and my daughters, I put on my performance personality and pushed through each day wearing a fixated smile on my face. I was determined to show my daughters the power of a woman having it all. On the outside looking in, it appeared I checked all the boxes. I looked good, my finances were being restored, my career was intact, and life went on. But In truth, it was all a façade. I was pushing to maintain that "all is well," but on the inside, deep in my soul, I was empty, exhausted, unfulfilled, and all alone. I was yearning for a connection to someone and to something that was lost. It felt like my soul was missing, my femininity and the juice of life was gone. I was hardhearted and tough-skinned, like I was the walking dead. I had lost me. The wear and tear began to take a toll on my physical and emotional health. It seemed as though my reign as queen had ended. My crown had fallen; it was tipped down and crooked. I was broken….nothing could put me back together.

One morning as I awoke, I was meditating on the hustle and bustle of the day ahead of me (getting the girls off to school, to dance lessons and basketball practices, all the meetings I had scheduled, appointments with clients, dinner prep—you know the list). I became overwhelmed and panicked. I remember one of my mantras that I live by to this day..."panic or pray."

So I began to pray. I dropped into my heart and cried out to God: "I can't do this anymore! Please come rescue me!" Something happened at that moment. An energy, a force, filled my heart. Peace and freedom came over me, although I was captured by the most tender, loving, small, still voice that began to speak to me. "Be still and know that I am God" (Psalm 46:10 NIV). There was a shift from my outer self to my inner soul self. I knew I had tapped into another part of my being. I began to drop inward to the Divine having its way with me. Tears began to flow and release, relief, and rescue happened. A remembering had come to my thoughts.The memory of God came to my still mind. I let go and a light was lit inside my being that melted all the madness, sadness, and brokenness away. There I was...WHOLE AND FULL. An internal peace and gentleness. I let out a sigh. I was home. Beautified in my brokenness.

In-lightened Beauty

That morning felt like a rebirth of my being. I was being showered and soaked in the presence of God's love and light. The more I visited this inner sanctuary, the more I began getting downloads of images and ideas. A renewed purpose for my life was coming into view. From this deep soul tending, I realized real beauty is finding your inner light—that spiritual connection with your feminine essence within, that essence that reveals the true deep passions and desires that God has designed for you. My soul was calling me up and out to the surface of my skin and to go deeper into the divine feminine beauty of myself and women. I met my true self, buried under family and cultural conditioning, other people's opinions of me, and inaccurate conclusions that I drew as a kid that became my beliefs about who I was. The truth set me FREE! I had a thriving cosmetic beauty business that tended to outer beauty, offering results in the form of a facelift, but now I was to guide women to a faithlift. To know, feel, and connect to the divine feminine within. The essence that God's Word refers to as the Holy Spirit within. Soulicious Lifestyle and Faithlift Coaching and Mentoring was born. I dove into scriptures, and God's Word became my new passion. I infused all my expertise in the field of physical beauty and fused it with the realm of spiritual beauty. Beginning with the most effective vitamins for external beauty care: Vitamins A, C, and E, and also for spiritual internal beauty care.

These are also three essential spiritual vitamins for the soul:

<u>Spiritual Vitamin A</u>: AWARENESS, AWAKEN, ALIGNMENT, ALLOWING

Awareness of this internal state of being is a main ingredient of Vitamin A and this aspect of you. One of my coined phrases in Soulicious is, "Those who don't go within…go without." In order to have an inner makeover, we must let go and drop into our inner being. It's amazing how many women are unaware and don't listen or feel this part of themselves is not real. When, in fact, it is the REAL self. The invisible YOU! The Soul Self. The soul always speaks to you…it never is not with you. God's Word says, "I will never leave you nor forsake you" (Hebrews 13:5 ESV). In order to hear it, we must be still and listen, as the Bible says, "for a small still voice." The problem with the world today is that we can all get too busy. It's as if being busy is the new trend. Having to be busy all the time is just a survival response to avoid dealing with trauma and unwanted emotions. But behind those unwanted emotions is a release and a beauty like no other. In order to deal with life, we must FEEL life. The good and the bad. A cleansing and exfoliation happens to the grit stuck to ourselves, and the soul is hydrated with the grace of the spirit and a freedom occurs. The Divine feminine wants to nurture you in the most mothering and tender way. It's referred to in the Bible as the "comforter", the "counselor", the "helper", and the "healer".

An **AWAKENING** and **ALIGNMENT** begins to occur within. **ALLOW** the light to ignite, rise and shine (See Matthew 5:16)...God says the light is "good" (Genesis 1:4 NIV).

Download the Soulself Profile at Souliciouslifestyle.com for a free sample of Spiritual Vitamin A .

In-Powered Beauty

Spiritual Vitamin C: **Clarity Confidence Courage**

Spiritual **clarity** is the perception and understanding that you are a child of God. You are the daughter of a King. Your Father is the King of the universe, so that makes you and I royalty. There is nothing that you are not, and there is nothing that you don't have. Let that soak in for a minute. Regardless of what you have been told about who you are or who you think you are not...get clear on your *true* identity. You are "beautifully and wonderfully made" (Psalm 139). Having clarity in your mind creates an inner-standing and ignites a strength and a presence within. Your inner immune system gets strengthened, and nothing can penetrate it.

Spiritual **confidence** simply means a trust within. The word itself reflects this: *Con* meaning "with" and *fidence* meaning "trust". I am talking about the kind of confidence of a woman who derives her strength from God's limitless power within her. A Godfidence. She knows that the same "Spirit of God, who raised Jesus from the dead, lives in" her (Romans 8:11 NLT). There is nothing that she can not do, be, have, or give. Beauty emanates from a woman who wears Soulicious confidence. She exudes a majestic presence of power and purpose, that of royalty. A queen.

Spiritual **courage**. Let's break down the word courage. *Cour* meaning "heart" and *rage* meaning "passion". Spiritual courage is simply living life from the passions in your heart. What are you passionate about? What makes you feel alive? What brings you joy? A sense of freedom and purpose? What makes you feel empowered? As women, we are programmed to put other people's needs before our own. Somehow our mothers and their mothers' mothers have brought the belief that women cannot live a life they love or that we "can't have it all." My mom told me to stop dreaming and that the life that I was divinely designed to have does not exist and that I was living in a fairy tale land. Ouch! She also told me about Santa Claus, and when I found out that he was not real, I simply stopped believing it. So, instead of doubting my dreams and desires, I simply stopped believing *her* and started believing in the LOVE that created me and who put me on Earth for a purpose. I am telling you the life God has for you, when you meet Him in your heart's desires, is happy, healthy, and holy (whole). It's up to you to undo all the lies and illusions of this world and have the courage to step out and walk with faith in your true beauty and brilliance. It takes courage to withstand the pains of self-discovery and let go of an old version of yourself. The authentic self is the soul self made visible. I can help support you in that journey in the Soulicious online course: "Dare to Desire" found on my website, Souliciouslifestyle/courses.

In-Bodied Beauty

<u>Spiritual Vitamin E</u>: Embrace, Embodied, Emerge

Once you are convinced and convicted about the truth of who you are, refusing to believe the lies (Santa Claus), it's time to **embrace** the new you, willingly and enthusiastically. You are a new creation; old things have passed away; behold, all things have become new" (2 Corinthians 5:17 NKJV). Wrap your arms around this new self and hold yourself closely with affection and admiration. Rest and settle into the rebirth process. Embracing your truth is essential to your purpose, power, and presence in this lifetime. To be the queen of your life, you must let your soul take a seat. You got this!

Once you have embraced the new beliefs it's time to **embody** your truth. To love the skin within you. Let the inner light glow brightly for all the world to see. Let this love and essence fill every cell in your body. Did you know your body is "God's temple and that God's spirit dwells in you? (1 Corinthians 3:16 ESV). Let this gorgeous, Godly, pure, effervescent energy reach the tip of your head entering the depths of your mind, all the way down to the depths of your soul. It will transform your soul. "Do not conform to the pattern of this world, but be transformed by the renewing of your mind" (Romans 12:2 NIV).

We are all embodied spirits, more spirit than body. We have been created in the image and likeness of God. Therefore we possess His very nature. It's in your DNA (Divine Natural Attributes)! We are to **emerge** as the spirit filled beings that we are in this material existence. To be in the world, but not of the world. As embodied spirits, we must develop our spiritual qualities and emerge with the spiritual essentials this world is needing, such as love, kindness, honesty, intellectual prowess, patience, and integrity. The Soulicious Woman emerges and rises. Within her is an essence not of this world. Though her purpose, power, and presence in this world is evident, she is here to build the Kingdom of God. She gracefully takes her seat as queen and owns her throne.

Here's the truth: We are all ROYAL. There are trials in our lives that are needed for, what I call "royal training" for the kingdom. The kingdom is your life. What you make of it. We are constantly changing and evolving, and sometimes that phase in your life will feel like you've lost your reign, like a breakdown but it's just an end to that stage. Our struggles are not meant to derail us but to deepen and strengthen us . All things are meant for our good. You've graduated, and God wants to take you Higher. To your Royal Highness. God has a perfect plan for your life and that plan is "to prosper you" and to "give you hope and a future" (Jeremiah 29:11 NIV). There is a Divine intelligence, a unique beauty, an amazing authentic truth that is within you and is seeking you. When you become aware and awakened to this essence of you, there is an activation of your personal power and purpose. A confidence and conviction emerges like no other. The inward journey is about finding your own fullness and giving yourself permission to have it. That thing we call intuition, it's your *soul*. You can trust it; it knows the way.

Align yourself with the truth within. Watch and see how magically life starts to flow with grace and ease. Opening up to the channel of your feminine freedom will magnify your beauty, goodness, and truth. You will begin to experience what it feels like to be fully expressed in your purpose with passion, presence and living a life you LOVE.

God has given you a kind of beauty that is internal and everlasting. Be Beauty, Be Full, Be Soulicious!

Take the quiz: Your Divine Essence

We all have unique gifts and talents that we're divinely given. Find out what your divine superpower is here:

https://www.souliciouslifestyle.com/divine-power-quiz.html

Get the Royal treatment. Skin Care for A Queen: Jafra.com/pamk

About the Author

Pamela Vatrano Kirastoulis is the creator and founder of Soulicious Lifestyle and Faithlift Coaching and Mentoring. She has a gift and passion for communicating to women all the different aspects of beauty. She has built a million-dollar sales team and beauty consulting business; she works with thousands of women. Over the past thirty-five years, she has helped women in the skin care and cosmetic industry achieve the beauty and success they desire. Pamela mentors, coaches, speaks and leads women in person and virtually through Soulicious Courses and Faithlift /Soulicious Bible studies for women. She has a unique style of fusing spiritual beauty and physical beauty into one. She believes that beauty and success are an inside job. She says, "Physical beauty is attractive, but spiritual beauty is captivating." Pamela believes pure beauty is elegance from the inside out and that there is nothing more beautiful and empowering than a woman who is comfortable in the skin she is in.

Connect with Pamela:
Email: Pamela@souliciouslifestyle.com
Website : Souliciouslifestyle.com
Website :Jafra.com/pamk

instagram.com/pamv_soulicious

FOURTEEN

Meredith Wilkie

LIFE ON THE EDGE OF DEATH

On a warm Perth evening, I took a train into the city to meet my friends. I was in for a fun night as they were in their early thirties and on trend with the finest dining spots and arty shows.

Having spent the past twenty years of my life in suburbia, and now divorced, I had moved closer to the city, and loved the pace, vibe, and a new world of experiences.

After a delicious meal, we set off to see a show. During the finale the entertainer invited the audience onto the stage area. Dancing and laughing, we were having the time of our lives. The stage by now resembled a mosh pit.

Without warning, my foot struck a speaker box lying on the floor. My legs swung out from under me, and I landed head-first with a massive thud onto the hard wooden bench seating.

My head flung back on impact, causing my jaw to move sharply to the right and my teeth to slash through my lower lip, deeply into the flesh. As I crawled up onto the bench in shock, I tasted shattered teeth debris and blood in my mouth.

I was raced to hospital and waited hours in the crowded emergency room to see a doctor. He explained,

'The cut is so deep I have no option but to use thick, nylon stitches. The wound will scar, but if you keep still, it will heal in a straight line.'

I interlaced my fingers with those of my handsome friend, took a deep breath and gripped it like a vice, shutting my eyes, scared to breathe as the doctor drove the needle into my lip and stitched the wound.

As the sun rose, my friend dropped me home. I walked dazed into my silent apartment, shut the door, dropped to the floor, and burst into tears.

I was too traumatised to sleep, and it was too early to call for support. I was alone and shaking. I opened a bottle of sparkling wine and sat

at my kitchen bench comprehending while sobbing my heart out.

What the hell had happened to me?

Exhausted, I showered and slipped into bed cuddling my fluffy polar bear for comfort. I woke at noon and looked into the mirror. I was horrified. The left side of my face was severely swollen and bruised. I stared at the huge nylon stitches across my lower lip and my bruised swollen left cheek.

My mouth hardly opened as it quivered and shook uncontrollably, and my jaw pulled to the right. I could merely mumble.

My general practitioner checked me over, gave me painkillers and arranged x-rays.

Resigned that this injury would take months of recovery, I was determined to get back to my old self again.

Or so I thought.

I was totally unprepared for the journey ahead. Initially dealing with a huge lump in my temporomandibular joint (TMJ) it was difficult to eat and talk. The splint I wore as I slept eased the pain and tension, dental visits smoothed off the broken teeth. I was referred to specialists for whiplash in my neck, constant tinnitus, and permanent hearing damage. All the while in unrelenting pain and discomfort.

A few weeks later the COVID19 pandemic hit. Isolation was a blessing, as it minimised daily activities that were physically and emotionally exhausting. Like the rest of the world, we were in lockdown. Working for the state government I was assigned duties to assist with the pandemic.

Christmas arrived and the city of Perth was COVID free. The state of Western Australia had its borders locked to the rest of the world. I was back at work but now the new norm was ZOOM calls. Businesses were in survival and recovery mode. This shielded me from the usual duties of my Business Development role pre-pandemic.

Christmas and New Year were tough. I was divorced, single and had no children. It also harboured the memory of losing my father on Christmas Day during a 12-month wave of intense grief that included the passing of my mother, my best friend and my Labrador.

This overlapping grief ultimately altered my perception of anticipating life events. The fear that anything could happen to sabotage plans was always present. My fortress walls were up, moat and all, to protect my heart from disappointment until the very last moment.

On Christmas Eve 2020 the sunbeams woke me with a tiny spark of hope. I had wonderful friends and some plans, so perhaps the draw-bridge could finally be lowered.

I attended an early appointment with a neurosurgeon as my head felt too heavy to hold upright for long periods of time.

Having been referred to a Professor of Neurosurgery, he had recommended I see a colleague who specialised in cranial injuries for a second opinion.

I walked into his office blindly optimistic. I had been consistent with my rehabilitation exercise, physiotherapy and felt strong and fit.

As I sat down, I could see x-rays on his monitor screen. He looked at me then said,

'You have a seven-millimetre flexion in the ligament that holds your head to your neck. It is normally three millimetres.'

I asked innocently,

'So, what does that mean?'

He explained,

'In this area of your vertebrae, C1 and C2, there is a very strong, thick ligament holding your head to your neck. You have cervical instability, as this ligament is literally hanging by a thread, pressing into the thecal sac around your spinal cord. If you have the slightest fall or accident it will result in penetrating the spinal cord, causing death or paralysis

Before the fear enveloped, I whispered, 'So, you can fix this, right?

'Yes, I can, but be aware the surgery is rare and major. You will permanently lose at least fifty percent of your head rotation. The surgery is millimetres from the brainstem and carotid artery, and there is a chance you may die, be a quadriplegic, or have a stroke during the surgery.

We'll fuse these joints together with bone cut from your iliac crest to form a paste. Then re-enforce the fusion with titanium screws and plates to secure the instability.'

The essence of my entire being spiraled downward into hopelessness. I was literally frozen with fear. My mouth slowly opened as I looked into his eyes in terror and burst into tears.

The C1 and C2 are the first two vertebrae at the top of the cervical spine. Together they form the atlantoaxial joint, which is a pivot joint, the major joint connecting your head to your neck allowing the head to rotate. This surgery is Category 1 – urgent, very high risk.

Due to the holiday season and extensive lists of pandemic surgery backlogs, February was the earliest date possible.

My niece, who is like a daughter to me, was getting married in February and it was my birthday on the 3 March. In a distorted state of fear, I chose the closest date that, should I die, I would leave this world having attended her wedding with a united family celebration to say goodbye and clicked over the last year of my life.

The surgery date was set for 11 March 2021.

He asked what I was doing for Christmas Day to get my mind off the enormity of the news.

I whispered, 'Going to yoga'.

His jaw dropped as he looked at me in astonishment and firmly stated my mum's childhood mantra,

'BE CAREFUL'

I walked out in a daze and sat in my car shaking and sobbing. *How? Why? What? This must be a mistake....* I speed-dialed the friend I knew had the ability to take my inner child from off the floor of hysteria to being able to function. She listened to my news between my hyperventilating sobs and slowly guided me safely back into a semi-functional state.

The Journey of Life on the Edge of Death had Begun

Until something life-threatening happens to you or within your closest circle, you listen with empathy. The degrees of separation protect you from the full enormity of emotions and understanding of walking in someone's shoes.

I have a fun adventurous spirit. Fit, healthy, and active, with a vibrant passion for life. I have travelled the world, hiked, zip-lined the highest mountains, rode the scariest roller coasters, parachuted with a free fall from fifteen thousand feet. Fearless!

I was now facing a period of 77 days of living on the edge of death in a state of unfathomable fear. The outcome of a slight trip or fall as I experienced every waking second. Terrified to live my life or to sleep with the fear of my head slipping off the pillow to dire consequences.

On top of this, there was no reassurance that I would even survive the surgery or not wake up as a quadriplegic.

Death or quadriplegic - if the ligament stretched a millimetre and the joint pressed into my spinal cord.

My long hair would be shaved to access the top vertebra with an incision made from the top of my skull to the base of my neck.

Bone carved from my iliac crest ground into cement for the fusion and the insertion of a permanent cage of titanium rods and screws for reinforcement.

We are talking 'Terminator', not ornate or pretty, but this head piece would save my life, so I decided to refer to it as my 'Crown'.

I asked my surgeon if all went well would I be able to ski? I had never skied and needed to visualise success and a kick ass goal.

I was back to yoga and gym having no idea of the minefield in my head. I had many angels protecting me.

This headspace ultimately led me to psychological support and to stop working. I was mentally and physically drowning.

My diagnosed post-traumatic stress disorder, depression, and anxiety from the incident were in overdrive. I was highly emotional and understandably terrified every minute of the day.

It was during this time that I had a huge light bulb moment: If I die, I will never have truly fulfilled my deepest desires and my life's purpose.

I was merely living, not actively stepping into creating the life of my dreams and expressing my full potential and calling.

I yearned for a balanced relationship with my true soulmate. Freedom to explore our own interests and goals but with deep trust, intimacy, support, joy, laughter, desire, and delicious 'can't get enough of each other' sex. I knew it existed. I had witnessed it and felt the potential on occasion, but it was always just out of reach.

The day of the surgery I felt numb and emotionless. I lay on the bed in my surgery gown pondering the enormity of what was ahead of me.

I was wheeled into a large operating theatre, crammed with machines and tools akin to a surgical horror movie. I looked into the eyes of my surgeon and pleaded,

'Please, don't let me die.'

Closing my eyes with images of skiing in fluffy fresh snow in Austria, I connected with my higher self. I then prayed to God and the universe:

'Guide him to do a perfect job and let me live'.

I awoke alarmingly, with the first thought to move my hands and legs. *I am not a quadriplegic.* Then asked the nurse - *all was well.*

I was euphoric, not just due to the copious amounts of opiates pumping into my system as this was in the top five most painful surgeries in the world. I had survived this surgery with the perfect outcome. I would never take the gift of my life lightly ever again.

The recovery was unbearable and aside from close friends and family popping in, and a freezer full of food thanks to a bestie, I was all alone.

My neck resembled a giant rolly dog. I felt as if my head had been decapitated then stuck back onto my neck, which was kind of accurate. I had no feeling on my skull, so when brushing my hair, I only felt the pull of the brush. I had a deep dent stitched in haste on my lower back and a long-stitched wound down my skull to the base of my neck.

Due to COVID my niece's wedding was rescheduled to a week after my surgery. This was such an important event in my life. Not being there on her special day with the small amount of family I had left mentally tipped me over the edge. I lay alone in my bed sobbing hysterically with fleeting thoughts of which narcotics I could take to go to sleep and never wake up. My cousin texted to say she was thinking of me, and my nephew sent me a photo he took just before the ceremony commenced with a message:

'The only thing missing is you'

His message gave me value and lifted me out of my pit of despair.

In the months ahead I put on a brave face, especially on social media, that I was normal and desirable - but could not shake feeling broken and disabled. No one would ever love me or want me. I was struggling with mental conditions, had a disfiguring scar on my lip, was unable to hear in certain situations, and in constant discomfort with the inability to turn my head more than 20 degrees.

Networking and social events with friends involved planning and psyching up for on my behalf. Discreetly arriving early to sit at the head of a table in a safe corner, or outdoors in a quiet controlled space that would not require me to turn my head, and which would enable me to hear and engage in conversations.

The sense of self-protection I had prior to the surgery, crossing the road, checking my blind spot driving, sitting on a chair or bench while turning to talk to people – gone. In a noisy crowded environment, I would have panic attacks and leave. I had no idea the fusion would affect my daily life so dramatically and take away my confidence and ability to feel safe.

My psychologist explained that it's difficult for people to understand or have empathy as your conditions are invisible. She said,

'To the world, you present as a beautiful, fit, sexy, capable woman. People are unable to know or see what lies behind the surface.'

I needed to find a way to move forward as behind the façade, I was sinking further down into a pit of depression and anxiety. I hid away in the safety of my home or spent time with my closest friends or family. God had given me this second chance and now it was up to me.

I thought that if I found my soulmate, I would be complete. Feeling so loved would give me the freedom to strive forward with my life's purpose. I had visualised how joyful I would feel and had put it out to the universe – so why was the universe not delivering?

The Destiny Pathway to Rise and Own My Crown

It was then that I had a massive 'Aha moment'. The deeper truth was I was not showing up in the vibe of my destiny. To connect to my soul's purpose and the soulmate of my dreams *'My King'* I must do the work to step up and raise my vibration to that of *a Queen*. I now had a Crown, so that was a start!

To fulfill my life's purpose, I must step boldly onto my destiny's path to manifest the future of my dreams. *But how?*

This involved a deep dive into my personal transformation and awakening journey. Identifying and breaking free from inner barriers, and cultivating new skills and capacities to nurture, develop and evolve.

I truly understood that my life's purpose was to utilise my unique experiences and knowledge. Now, infused with personal relatability and deep understanding, to share challenges and insights from living on the edge of death and surviving. To inspire and coach other women ultimately to step up to discover their unique calling and live their best lives and never to leave this life with their song unsung.

I enrolled in a Feminine Power course which led me to becoming a Certified Transformational Life Coach. Dr Claire Zammit's brilliance resonated with me to awaken the power to create what I yearned for and to fully awaken my authentic feminine power to create the destiny of my dreams.

I have always been fascinated by tales of Kings and Queens, palaces and far away kingdoms. My home is adorned with crowns so perhaps in an odd way I manifested mine.

Little girls dream of being Princesses, and Disney portrayed them as the most beautiful and desired by many handsome knights.

While delving into my authentic feminine archetype I resonated with the energy of a Queen – no mere knights for me but a strong, masculine equal – *a King*.

This led me to align with the energetic vibration of *a* Queen, peaceful in her authentic serenity.

She makes present her needs and expectations to others and remains open to change and opinion. She trusts curiously and playfully that all of life and the universe have her back. When challenges arise, she reacts from a place of love, and learns and grows.

Aware her very existence is enough to attract her King with her curiosity, openness, and receptivity, she lets go of masculine energy and turns towards her deepest feminine desires.

She is open hearted and champions others, knowing she is connected to her higher self and to life universally.

I now 'Own My Crown' – both physically and metaphorically.

The purpose for sharing my story is to inspire you to never lose hope in the face of adversity. To act now, and dive into your destiny and follow your heart. To share your unique calling with the world and to step up to the throne of your life.

About the Author

Meredith Wilkie is a Women's Transformational Life Coach who draws from her personal reflections and terrifying challenges of Living on The Edge of Death to inspire women to rise to their greatness and thrive in the face of adversity. With over 25 years as a health, fitness, and wellness professional her coaching, personal training methods, classes and workshops have influenced and changed the lives of thousands of women.

As a presenter, author, and coach with a passion for the archetypal vibration of a Queen she inspires energy, power, confidence, and femininity to live life to the full. Meredith advocates for self-love and resilience with poise and grace. She encouragers women to step forward into their destiny to Own their Crown, follow their calling and step up to the throne of their lives. She provides hope, strength, and inspiration that from the darkest of nights can appear the brightest of diamonds.

Meredith lives in Perth, Western Australia, and spends her time traveling or enjoying the company of her family and friends, 42-degree hot yoga classes or in the company of her gorgeous rag doll cat, Coco. She is fascinated by iconic bridges, crowns, and the magnificence of big old trees and is motivated to fulfill her dream goal of skiing in Austria.

Website: ownyourcrown.au
Contact: meredithwilkie.com.au

FIFTEEN

Sonja Wüthrich

SOUL COMMUNICATION EXCELLENCE: THE TREASURE OF OUR SOUL

There is no deeper language you can learn to listen to and finally express, than that of your soul. In doing so, you learn to connect to the deep language of other souls. Even if they are different in expression, the source is always one and the same for all beings. – Sonja

Why Do We Need Soul Communication?

Understanding the ways of communication that our soul uses to express its perception of life deeply fascinates me. The reason lies in my personal story and in my spiritual gifts. As a highly sensitive soul I have been blessed with clairvoyant and visionary insights, as well as clairaudience and clairsentience abilities, since my early childhood. Learning to understand my "clairs" built the basis for my life. It became crucial for my wellbeing to understand and take care of the way my soul is sharing its wisdom with the world.

Women are about to open-up to and discover their "clairs". This is a phenomenon that is closely connected to the healing and ascension journey we are on. Conscious enfolding and use of our "Soul's

Communication Excellence" helps us to finally shine as the beautiful feminine ascension artists, healers and leaders of our time.

Our soul is in constant communication with life and thus with us. A conscious handling of this flow of communication provides us with confidence, heightens our consciousness, and activates our natural self-healing power. Consequently, listening to and expressing our soul's language has a positive influence on our physical and non-physical health.

In the summer of 2018, my own Soul Communication Excellence started to shine in a new light. I received visions, evoked from a personal to a super-personal level. Overarching visions came through, directed to mankind, and at that time, especially, to womankind. The following vision about the Feminine Creator came through in late summer 2018. It opened a whole new chapter of my life. Its content is clearly directed to us, the women of today:

A woman's body floating wide up in the blue sky, beautiful, large, and impressive. She is completely white, made of an essence comparable to a fusion of air and water. A dreamlike liquid, implying a sense of a vivid dust. The sparkling of millions of little diamonds, inheriting the possibility of being everything.

She is ageless and timeless. Her eyes are closed, but her restless sleep indicates wild dreaming. It seems as if she is just about to create herself. The state she is in, is reminiscent of an empty canvas.

Suddenly, her dust-like body cracks open. Thousands of little milky-white butterflies, made of her own kind, are rising from her lower belly. They dance and move higher, and after a moment full of sparkling magic, they swarm out into one direction. It looks like they are heading out to collect their own colors in order to return later to her beautiful white body and to fill it up with an immense orchestration of colors.

On the horizon the feeling arises that it is now up to her to accept her purpose: to create a New Femininity, which is colorful and magical. Once she is ready, the numerous white butterflies will return to help her.

This vision shows each of us women that the timing is right to take care of her – in each of us. She helps us to see what the time asks from us: to be the most wonderful, gifted, talented, and awakened artists, healers or leaders we can be. The blue of the sky around her is welcoming her presence. This fresh and white Feminine Creator Being is giving birth to what her heart wished for ages ago: a new life, colorful, sensitive, humane, and feminine. Now more than ever, is she preparing herself to co-create with us. It feels so right and promising, as she is us, as well as we are her.

My Awakening Story

The colors of the tree, yellow, red, and brown, enlighten my soul. It is early November, and the days are getting remarkably short. This is the time of the year that I loved as a child. My visit home is special to me as I am reminded of my own feminine awakening story.

I was always aware that my mother decorated the house and garden with butterflies and dragonflies. But on that November morning I realized that her decoration has more to do with me than I ever noticed before. Even her remarkable collection of drawings and paintings of women correlate with a main topic of my life: the feminine brilliance. All these women, without exception, were drawn in sensitive, calm positions. They all bare a magical glow in their aura. A glow evoked by an intimate moment of being unobserved.

Among these women, painted with oil and watercolor and drawn in charcoal, I spot my own portrait in an angle of my mother's bedroom. The drawing is surrounded by more women, all obviously selected with care and love.

The fine lines of my face are drawn by a careful but secure hand. I remember the artist well. She was in her sixties, it must be over twenty years back, while I was working as a model for a group of artists. She was full of confidence, filled with a nice spirit. I spotted wisdom in her eyes while she observed me, ready to lead the pencil over the drawing paper.

Later, when I looked at my portrait, it showed a sensitive, vulnerable but obviously powerful woman in her early twenties. I saw confidence in my eyes but also a certain reservedness. As if I anticipated that a lot of strength would be needed on my path ahead. Strength to find my freedom and self-confidence; strength to express and share the wisdom that my soul bears. A wisdom that supports my desire for the mission I brought into life.

I well remember how I accepted her invitation. She handed her card over to me when she, late at night, left the atelier. She intended to gift me with a copy of the drawing.

She lived close to the center of the main town of the region I lived. Her flat was clean and cozy, but too small for all the furniture and the hundreds of books sitting on her shelves. I understood that she knew the content of the books; I didn't even need to ask her. We were sitting in her living room, the window wide open. I spotted the sun through passing white clouds. Some sunrays were reflected on the table's surface, smooth as glass.

We enjoyed a cup of hot tea. She amused me with pleasant but also intense episodes of her life. She was an inspiring communicator, and it was fun listening to her. Suddenly, she turned around to grab a book from the shelf behind her. With a smile on her face, she placed it in front of me, mentioning that the content would be interesting to me. The book was science-based but the content was mystic. I remember well the long text passages but also pictures that took me on a journey of traces from old civilizations, landscapes or continents. Some of them are not even existing anymore on the map of the world as we know it today - like Atlantis. She obviously sensed my interest in mystical and spiritual topics. I remember how these pictures and passages alerted my senses in an unusual way while I was thumbing through the pages.

Years later a good friend commented on this encounter with the phrase: "This beautiful feminine artist saw the real and ancient priestess in you." She was right.

From the moment I left her house, gifted with a copy of my portrait, I realized that something had changed in me. I knew my spiritual gifts already since my childhood. For years, mostly in my early adulthood, I carefully tried to hide and deny them for the sake of preserving my own safety. But now it felt like this woman's energy had opened up these sacred gifts in me. Gifts that I had forgotten for a long time.

The following weeks, I started to feel and see energies, beings or situations that were not visible to others. I felt hidden reasons behind events, and I started to hear voices, not audible to people around me. I was a bit confused about the insights. But since what I heard and saw was good and full of wisdom, I tried to relax.

As a child I was extra sensitive, and a quick learner. On many levels I was busy as a bee processing the feelings, thoughts, and unspoken words from people around me. Looking back, I see myself literally absorbing information from conversations led by people around me. I intuitively understood the expectations from my environment. For me, the unspoken words were as valuable and powerful as the spoken ones. I realized quickly that delivering on unspoken expectations from others made my way and life much easier and so I developed into a caring and giving soul. That I had a ton of natural light to spread and give to others, was another reason why sharing it was easy for me. My natural assumption was that we are all the same.

My identity felt complete, still deeply bonded to the place of light it came from. I had no other tools than my own light to illuminate my path into the world.

It is often the case that human beings with these outstanding intuitive perceptions are standing alone within their environment; so was I. Naturally and quietly, I accessed my "clairs". They made me aware that I was more mature and showed more emotional intelligence than most people around me.

In my younger years, visions gave me insights into the true being of people; it happened that even if I didn't know a person, I saw her or his true being. I saw it shining in another dimension behind the person's physical body. The insights and the information that flowed in my visions I soaked up like a precious liquid. They were my natural connection to Source. In these moments the space around me felt like an ocean of information. It was natural for me to see, read, and understand it.

In my younger adulthood, I understood that the world around me was not representing my inner reality. The linearity in which the world around me lived, strongly limited my abilities. I started to accept linearity as truth, and aimed to fit in and be a part of this reality. My holistic intelligence, my "clairs", as well as my natural abilities to connect and co-create with Source faded, until they were nearly gone.

But only because of this single visit at the artist's home, my spiritual gifts got back "online". My senses became alert much faster than before. My entire perception shifted to a higher vibrational, more sensitive level. Sure, ordinary life had trained me to push my senses down. But now the wheel was turned on and I could neither control the direction nor the intensity of the spin it took. I also had no chance to further control the bumpiness of the road I got on from this point in my life. On the soul level an alchemical process of change was kicked off and started to take the lead.

Without really noticing it, I started to question the path I was on. My soul went on a journey to find more depth, strength, wisdom - more of me. My higher self needed more sparkle than my regular life and current relationships provided me with.

Dissatisfaction, a certain pinch of unhappiness started to be the undesirable companion at my side, causing stress in and around me. Up-till-then stable and harmonic relationships started to scramble slowly.

What followed were painful break ups and parting with loved ones and friends who had been with me for years. I had no clue how to reorganize myself with the new desires that had opened inside of me. My clairaudience and clairvoyance pulsed louder and louder. I even felt persecuted at times. Slowly but surely, I fell out of balance. But instead of listening and stepping back, I grasped at straws: like new lovers that appeared on the horizon.

So one and a half years later, I found myself heartbroken, emotionally destroyed, disorientated, and extremely unhappy and depressed at the end of just another non-heart-centered relationship. I was twenty-three years old, and my heart was lost. I had no idea what I needed in relationships, in my profession, or in friendship. I was unable to see any path to go on. I needed a break; so, I left my home village and took time off.

I felt so deeply broken that I only had two choices: to quit and end life or to start to seriously and carefully listen to my soul. I decided to listen deeply. I carefully took notes of what my "clairs" let me hear and see. I developed a new interest in my spiritual gifts and slowly I found a new acceptance for them. I decided to train myself and practice daily as I learned that disrespecting these instruments could have fatal consequences for my wellbeing.

I looked for literature around my spiritual abilities and I learned that I am not alone with these gifts. I realized slowly that being different is the unique foundation of my I AM. For the first time in my life, I courageously started to stand on my own perceptions.

On all levels of my being, I noticed changes. As if I were growing slowly into the architecture of my being. My self-confidence grew as I started to breathe in my own light. There was still a journey in front of me. But at least I knew where I didn't want to end up again.

I understood that our thoughts have the power to create feelings, and that our feelings have the power to create thoughts. What really leads us, however, is the heart, and I learned to respect it.

A new ease was reflected in my mood and days. I succeeded in taking my power back and sorting things out in my life without the constant need to figure it out with my head; my heart took slowly over. My "clairs" fascinated me, as they made me special, and I fell in love with myself for the first time in my life.

I felt the urge to be authentic, and I loved to stand behind all my spiritual gifts. This was the moment when Cyndie, the founder of Feminine Mastery, and the five Feminine Archetypes, stepped into my life. I loved Cyndie and my inner child was glowing for the Archetypes and their brilliance. My abilities got even more tangible as I established deep friendships with women who are similar in heart and soul, while being all grounded in their uniqueness. I felt loved with all my outstanding abilities and with my hunger for excellence. My understanding, admiration, and love for womanhood grew exponentially. I realized how powerful women are when we support each other in this process to honor our brilliance and to heal our wounds.

I clearly identified with the Feminine Archetype of the Dragonfly. That day visiting the home of my childhood, I was touched when I realized that the dragonfly was decorating the house of my parents years before I knew about Feminine Mastery and the five Feminine Archetypes.

Today, I am aware that my awakening story is a gift not only for myself but also for the women of my lineage and for womanhood itself. As the intuitive and powerful woman that I am I had to understand our feminine story the feminine way. Looking back, I see that I prepared all my early life for my awakening as a young woman. My soul waited to get the right signs, in order to step out of the life I was embedded in, and to spread her wings.

Ignoring or refusing our soul-language is one of the most hurtful acts we can do to ourselves. Our physical, mental, and spiritual bodies answer for our disrespectful treatment. We might feel rising depression, fears of all kinds, feelings of emptiness, lack or brokenness. A deep knowing I gained from this time is that we pay a heavy price if we decide not to be who we really are! But when we have the courage to listen deeply and with care, we find a treasure of gold.

What Is Soul Communication Excellence?

Souls naturally drive for excellence in expression. While we are awakening our Soul's Communication Excellence, the ascending artist, healer and leader that we are, blooms into its full beauty. – Sonja

Soul Communication is always active on all levels of our being; hence, there is no way not to communicate. It is wise and increasingly efficient to learn to master this kind of communication. Understanding how our soul constantly communicates with life is the path to Soul Communication Excellence. With the right tools and support at hand, we can fast track learning and expressing our soul's language.

Life reacts well to our soul's way of communicating with its surroundings. If you get more sensitive and attentive to the various forms of answers that life provides, your confidence in being well-guided in life grows exponentially. Our gifts and soul talents respond fast when our soul's language gets the required attention.

Soul Communication has the positive power to feed and caress our senses. It is built on our soul's universal wisdom. The depth of our being is a mystical unknown, but its source is the Divine Self and the one and only Source of Truth itself. In the void, the zero point where creation of all things starts, our soul's language flows most authentically. When we learn to consciously connect to the zero point, we find our deepest attention and highest intentions well-bundled.

Soul Communication Excellence is a flow that resonates with our spiritual gifts, the exceptional non-physical senses, named as clairaudience, clairsentience, clairvoyance, clairessence, clairgustance, and claircognisance. Visions, for example, are talking in a silent language that intuitive sensations powerfully catch through dimensions beyond time and space.

"Clairs" are interconnected, and they support each other to bring the message through for the open and trained in mind and heart person. Each of us can learn to orchestrate their perception on physical and non-physical levels. That way, "clairs" are able to support the extension of our consciousness. They help us to receive the non-linear information originating from our soul's talk with life, through the quantum space.

How Does This Awareness Support People?

Throughout my career as a teacher, coach, and intuitive healer, I've had the chance to lead sensitive souls of all ages and genders through intense life transformation processes. One common topic that many sensitive souls share, is how to find a way to gain back trust in their soul's guidance.

The flatness of the reality we currently live in can cause an insecurity in sensitive souls about their own perception. In addition, it might make us doubt and put us under stress about how successfully we are integrated into this life and our place and tribe in it.

Because one of the strengths of highly intuitive people is the ability to adapt to the environment. That adaptation can be so strong and successful that you might be feeling like losing your identity beyond recognition, even for yourself.

This loss of connection to one's identity causes imbalances in various areas of our life. To ease your path, you must re-establish the unique way of your perception.

Awakening your Soul Communication Excellence brings you peace and connection. For it enables each of us to consciously balance and heal our inner feminine and masculine. If we are in harmony with ourselves, we lay the foundation for more peace between each other. This is the peaceful moment when we do not need to mirror each other's wounding anymore.

The Feminine Soul Communication Healing Archetypes

Everything that really matters to us, starts with the awareness of the identity of our soul. Having set this foundation, our purpose and what we love to share with the world gets clear. Our self-confidence raises. This empowerment is a door-opener for the magic and the bliss of love for oneself and for life. – Sonja

I began to receive transmissions of the *StarlightMedicine Immersion (SMI)* in 2018. Since then the Transmissions are powerfully growing within me and the women in my field through our awakening processes. The Transmissions connect us with the unique and rich starlight essence that we are. The essence contains all we have ever needed, since the beginning of our time.

The *Sacred Feminine Soul Communication System (SFSCS)* is part of the *StarlightMedicine Immersion (SMI)*. It holds our feminine evolution and awakening processes. The eighteen Healing Archetype Goddesses of the *SFSCS* are beautiful guides and coaches for our Soul Communication Excellence. With them we can raise up, heal, and grow in safety, and in accordance with our individual needs.

Our starlight holds our primal soul message. If we understand the message and messenger that we both are, the Archetype Goddesses help us spread our wings to share the message with the world. They help us to bring our unique life expression out from the hidden spaces into the shining light.

Each of the Goddess sisters carries her own healing secrets, that she mainly works with. They surround us with their unique sphere and lead us to find answers within. They have a joyful way of stimulating our abilities to listen to our soul. Moreover, they activate our self-healing forces while they sweeten our journey of self-discovery.

A special beauty of the Goddesses lies in their names. They stand for natural qualities that express our feminine nature. We are about to build a New Femininity, and these qualities are all part of it.

I am now presenting six of the eighteen Healing Archetype Goddesses to spread their love and precious healing secrets:

Six Healing Archetype Goddesses from the *SFSCS*

The Archetype Goddess Joy

Primal Medicine of the Universe & Ultimate Motivation – The recalibration to the frequency of Joy and happiness provokes beautiful universal and miraculous fast-track reactions. Joy recharges our system. She deeply motivates us on our self-healing and self-discovery path. Also she helps us overcome dry and lean periods. Joy masters and dissolves the illusionary, uncalm, and hardened spirit of our pain bodies, created on our path.

The Archetype Goddess Consciousness

Soul Communication & Soul Compass – The *Sacred Feminine Soul Communication System (SFSCS)* is a celebration of the art of intuition and soul-expression. Consciousness, at the matching higher level of frequency, is an inherent compass that provides us with an orientation in the quantum field. She leads us home safely. As life is a constant flow of communication, she trains our receiver instruments, such as our inner guidance, the intuition, to get eloquent in reading, translating, and expressing the sacred languages.

The Archetype Goddess Vitality

Transformation of Energy & Finding Balance in Body, Mind and Spirit – Everything is energy. The transformation of energy is the basis for all changes in life. Vitality brings balance in our body, mind and spirit. She orchestrates our breath, and holds the space between everything. She carries our holy flame of life, the wise light of our soul. She plays with the energy of the water we are made of, that keeps everything connected. And finally, she caresses the earth, the matter that is basis for our physical form.

The Archetype Goddess Compassion

Love is The Highest Living Light & the Power of Truth, Humility, and Thankfulness – Compassion raises where a true, sacred, and nonjudgmental space is held. What is seen and accepted through the eyes of unconditional love and empathy can finally heal. Through the connection to the Divine Self, we become active players in the sacred architecture of life and of love's evolutionary process. If we walk consciously on the ground of love in practicing humility and thankfulness, we walk close beside the mystical streams of life. They constantly feed our soul and spirit through the life we live.

The Archetype Goddess Passion

Metamorphosis & The Phoenix – Moving from pain to beauty is the process of dying and re-birthing into life. Passion brings the flame of life to the most hidden endpoints in our soul. These are the places where we have hidden our holy wings. If she rises with us like a Phoenix, we turn from anger to fruitful changes. She transforms grief into empathy and life force. She leads us out of fear into courage. Passion knows how to turn rage into self-determination. She changes self-pity into self-esteem and she guides us from being broken-hearted into a state of hope and positive expectation. Our tears are the holy connection in between.

The Archetype Goddess Strength

Feminine Superpowers & Uniqueness of Being – What is seen in the eyes of true love grows beyond measure. With her, the path of self-healing and self-discovery eases while we feel safer and safer to grow into our full size. We recognize our superpowers, and we focus and express ourselves through the uniqueness we are.

THANK you from my heart for listening to my story and the magic of the above six Archetype Goddesses, the *StarlightMedicine Immersion (SMI)* and the *Sacred Feminine Soul Communication System (SFSCS)*.

If you're interested in receiving a free gift with the divine healing abilities of all eighteen Archetype Goddesses get it here:

www.sonjawuethrich.com.

Under the same website you can request a free "Your Archetype Goddesses-Breakthrough Session" or send my your questions or feedback. I am happy to hear from you.

The Goddesses and I are blessing you.

Much Love and Light,

Sonja

About the Author

Sonja Wüthrich is a highly sensitive intuitive healer, coach, and soul communication expert. She lives and works in Switzerland. Over three decades Sonja has supported children, young adults, women, and men of all ages to find a healthy balance in their relationship to life. Sonja has been gifted with extraordinary talents of clairvoyance, clairaudience, and clairsentience since her childhood. This high sensitivity enables her to reconnect her clients with the uniqueness of their soul expression. This is also at the core of her healing and coaching work. She joyfully leads people to create their life in alignment with their soul's deepest expression.

Between 2018 to 2020 Sonja received the deeply mystical Transmission of the *StarlightMedicine Immersion* through a series of visions. The Transmission contained various healing modalities which intuitively support people on their path of self-healing and self-discovery. The deep *Immersion* modalities train people in an intuitive way to carefully listen to the mystical communication of their soul and this enables them to constantly keep up with life. Part of the system are "The Healing Archetypes", "The Resort", "The Pulse of Life", and "The Cosmic Universal Pharmacy", amongst others. The goal of her work is to free up the expression of our soul's mystic language. That way we find our natural sovereignty, health, and happiness.

In this book Sonja reveals how her own feminine awakening brought her to the understanding that there is no deeper language than that of our soul. Soul-language is a key to understanding what happens in us and around us. We can learn to listen to and express this deep language, and when we do listen to it, it gifts us with a juicy, intimate, and loving relationship with ourselves and with the Source of all life.

Sonja's career reflects that she can bridge worlds. She has worked as a certified teacher, and has established a private school for children and young adults. For a decade she built up the LISTE The Young Art Fair promoting young international artists and galleries in giving them a platform to sell their work. She is certified as a life and transformation coach. She practices as an intuitive healer using various healing modalities, like *StarlightMedicine Immersion*, Spontaneous Transformation technique and the Biofield Immersion technique. She is also a skilled, certified senior project manager, PMP, with over twelve years of experience in running global programs in the industry. She works as a flexible and inspiring leader and a confident communicator. She has proven ability to successfully manage all facets of projects of various industry branches. Her extraordinary ability to work with people are clearly enhanced by her experience in the science of education and coaching and by her exceptional spiritual gifts.

Website: www.sonjawuethrich.com / www.starlightmedicine.com
Email: info@sonjawuethrich.com

Acknowledgments

Thank you to the entire Soul Excellence Publishing Team for helping make this book a reality!

To **Kristina Brummer** for spearheading all author communication, collecting all author chapters, bios, and headshots and for keeping everything on time and running smoothly.

To **Kelly Fischer** of Depth Theory for designing all of the colorful and inspiring marketing graphics and copy for the book and summit and making it easy for the authors to share it with their networks.

To **Natalie Gleason** for formatting the book, overseeing cover design, and preparing all assets to publish on Amazon.

To **Rosemi Mederos** for all of her editing expertise, guiding the authors through their chapter edits, and helping them to make their story the best it could be.

To **Sol Muñoz** for leading The Queen Bee Summit and helping guide all the authors through the preparing, scheduling, promoting, and delivering of their transformational talks.

And to **all the amazing women** in this book.

And to you, **dear reader**, thank you!

About Soul Excellence Publishing

Amplifying the Wisdom of Conscious, Courageous Leaders

Founded in September 2020 by Kayleigh O'Keefe, after working with the Divine Feminine Archetypes of Feminine Mastery, Soul Excellence Publishing has quickly built a reputation for helping over 350 executives, entrepreneurs, and community leaders share their authentic selves in best-selling books, such as:

- *Leading Through the Pandemic: Unconventional Wisdom from Heartfelt Leaders*
- *Significant Women: Leaders Reveal What Matters Most*
- *The X-Factor: The Spiritual Secrets Behind Successful Executives & Entrepreneurs*
- *The Great LeadHERship Awakening*
- *The Diversity in Humanity: A New Vision for Creating Harmony in the Workplace*
- *Black Utah: Stories from a Thriving Community*
- *STEM Century: It Takes a Village to Raise a 21st-Century Graduate*

Website: https://soulexcellence.com

About Feminine Mastery

Discover the woman you were born to be

Feminine Mastery is a global movement of women who are embodying their truth and living fully expressed.

If you are on the path to self discovery and yearn for a meaningful life fulfilled with your dreams, you are in the right place. Once you express and embody your true self, the life meant just for you unfolds naturally and abundantly. This is a universal truth that has been kept a secret from women until now!

Our Feminine Mastery Path has made what was once a secret into a proven solution to expressing yourself and manifesting your dreams too. Discover your Feminine Mastery Mentor Archetype by taking the quiz that has been taken by over 30,000 around the globe.

https://femininemastery.com/quiz/

Made in the USA
Monee, IL
06 May 2023